BLUE COLLAR RESISTANCE AND THE POLITICS OF JESUS

BLUE COLLAR RESISTANCE

AND THE

POLITICS OF JESUS

Tex Sample

Doing

Ministry

with

Working

Class

Whites

ABINGDON PRESS
NASHVILLE

BLUE-COLLAR RESISTANCE AND THE POLITICS OF JESUS
DOING MINISTRY WITH WORKING-CLASS WHITES

Copyright © 2006 by Abingdon Press

All rights reserved.

This book is printed on acid-free paper.

Library of Congress Cataloging in Publication Data

Sample, Tex.
  Blue-collar resistance and the politics of Jesus : doing ministry with working-class whites / Tex Sample.
    p. cm.
  Includes bibliographical references.
  ISBN 0-687-33502-7 (pbk. : alk. paper)
  1. Church work with the working class—United States. 2. Working class whites—Religious life—United States. I. Title.

  BV2695.W6S365 2006
  259.086'23—dc22

                                                        2006016604

Scripture quotations are from the *New Revised Standard Version of the Bible*, copyright 1989, Division of Christian Education of the National Council of the Churches of Christ in the United States of America. Used by permission. All rights reserved.

Chapters 1–4 were first published in *Currents in Theology and Mission* in 2000. Reprinted by permission.

06 07 08 09 10 11 12 13 14 15 – 10 9 8 7 6 5 4 3 2 1
MANUFACTURED IN THE UNITED STATES OF AMERICA

CONTENTS

Acknowledgments vii

Chapter 1: Pitching Tent in the World of Class 1

Chapter 2: The Practices of Class 13

Chapter 3: The Practices of Resistance 31

Chapter 4: Faith Commitment of the Heart 49

Chapter 5: The Politics of Jesus 65

Chapter 6: The Craft Tradition of Discipleship 85

Chapter 7: The Social Witness of the White
           Working-class Church 105

Notes 127

ACKNOWLEDGMENTS

The first four chapters of this book were originally given in an oral and multimedia form as the Hein Fry Lectures of 2000. I was one of the two lecturers that year and delivered these lectures at four of the seminaries of the Evangelical Lutheran Church in America: The Lutheran Northwestern Theological Seminary, The Lutheran School of Theology at Chicago, The Lutheran Theological Southern Seminary, and The Pacific Lutheran Theological Seminary. I am grateful for the warm hospitality I received at each of these schools and for the many good conversations in which I was engaged by faculty and students around these events. The lectures were subsequently published in *Currents in Theology and Mission* (28, 2). Published by the Lutheran School of Theology at Chicago in cooperation with Pacific Lutheran Theological Seminary and Wartburg Theological Seminary, (April, 2001): 110-37. I am grateful to Ralph W. Klein, editor of *Currents in Theology and Mission*, for his invaluable help in putting the lectures in print form.

While I am finally responsible for the views and claims of this book, I am indebted to friends who read the manuscript and to significant contributions others have made. Gene Barnes and Karen Spencer-Barnes gave it the critical eye of those who work professionally in the church. I appreciate their friendship and their thoughtful readings of the manuscript. I also appreciate a number of conversations I had with Gilbert H. Caldwell and William B. McClain about white working-class people, especially in light of more recent political events at the national level. I appreciate especially their assurances that concerns addressed here are important. No one has more affected my study of working-class Americans than Larry Hollon. Our team teaching and work together across the years on working people, especially in relationship to country music, is a major contribution to everything I do here.

This is the second book I have done at Abingdon Press with Robert Ratcliff as my editor. I appreciate his eye for needed additions to the text and for his good spirit in conversations about it. It is a pleasure and a blessing to work with him.

Peggy Sample is my best friend and our lives are so fully engaged with each other that I cannot think of anything I do that is not shaped by her and made better by her generosity and clarity of soul.

Chapter 1

PITCHING TENT IN THE WORLD OF CLASS

F ive years ago the Reverend J. L. "Tubs" Larkin went to a working-class church in an urban neighborhood in a large metropolitan city. The church had 200 members and about a hundred in attendance. The membership was made up of families of autoworkers, small-factory workers, and a diverse range of service occupations. After Tubs had visited his members and conferred with his board, he made changes in the worship service, doing away with as much reading as he could and making use of oral practices with the liturgy. He did what the congregation called *Bible preaching*, in which he focused on the biblical text but drew helpful analogies for the lives of the people in the church. His preaching style was basically storytelling with a use of many memorable sayings. The worship service drew on music and hymns that the people liked while making sure they were theologically sound. Soon after his arrival and after several good discussions at the board meeting, the church began practicing the Eucharist every Sunday. Communion was brief, about ten minutes, and used basically the words of institution and an interpretation of the centrality of the Lord's Supper that emphasized the congregation as the body of Christ. He spoke often of the fact that in the Eucharist there is no room for anyone lording it over someone else. Meanwhile in the church school he began an emphasis on apprenticeship learning and focused on skills that Christians need to know to be faithful.

His pastoral work focused on helping people cope, struggle, and survive but doing so as people in a church that increasingly saw themselves as a family. It is also interesting what he did not do. He did not preach family systems theory, Myers-Briggs, pop psychology, or make other moves that focused on the subjectivity of his congregation. When he used such things, they were in the background of what he did, not the focus of his attention.

Tubs was continually on the lookout for opposition that cropped up here and there. He especially attempted to avoid drawing the congregation's covert opposition by imposing or suggesting business or professional practices that reminded them of their bosses and work situations. When and where he found resistance, he did everything he could to dissolve it by taking sides anytime he could with the people doing the resistance. Sensitive to the ways in which working people are demeaned at work and in the wider community, he was careful to show respect to people and to watch out not to engage in behavior that looked like what working people encounter that demeans them, their tastes, their talk, their very world.

The community was also his parish. He got himself invited to a couple of union halls and actively attended social functions, and later worked with them as chaplain. With the understanding and support of his church board, he visited regularly a bar and a beer hall in the community. While in these places he never drank alcohol, explaining that he was "working." Mainly he just built ties with people there, and after a couple of years conducted two weddings for people from the beer hall. A few people from both drinking establishments now attend his church.

Indigenous Practices and Pitching Tent

Tubs in his ministry does what I call "pitching tent." The phrase "pitching tent" comes from the Gospel of John 1:14, where it says, "The Word became flesh and lived among us." The word *lived* here is a translation of the Greek word *skeenoo*, which literally means "pitched tent."[1] This claim is central to the incarnation, and I read this to mean that Jesus as the Word of God joined the indigenous practices of his time. "Pitching tent" was an indigenous practice in his time. It was a fundamental way of taking up habitation with people. Yet, he "pitched tent" metaphorically in a host of ways. He was a carpenter, an occupation in the culture of his time. He went to the marginal people of his world, who were illiterate, and he taught them in parables. He was a faithful Jew and participated in central practices of his faith, although he also opposed some of those practices. He spoke Aramaic, thus taking up the language of his people. His teaching used images from that world in terms of lilies, fish, sowing and reaping, mustard seeds, the weather, and much more. The church as the body of Christ must take this kind of language and these kinds of practices very seriously.

I contend that there has never been an authentic expression of Christian faith that was not also indigenous. In fact, serious tragedy attends the missionary work of the church when it refuses to be indigenous. I think here of the missionaries who prohibited Native Americans from bringing the drum into worship. The same is true of the missionary work with African Americans who were forbidden to worship with the drum. The result for them was that their hands and feet became percussive so that indigenous cadence and rhythm were not lost to the praise and glorification of God. To pitch tent is intrinsic to the incarnate activity of a Triune God made known in Christ who works through the Spirit. One task of the church as the body of Christ in the world is to instantiate such incarnational activity.

The focus on practices is central to my work. I am very much interested in indigenous practices, but I am also very interested in the practices that are intrinsic to the Christian faith—for example, the Eucharist. It is our job to respond to God's Word and to pitch tent with the practices that are indigenous to a people. But this does not mean we pitch tent with every practice. Some practices are to be resisted and the church is to be an alternative to such practices. Such discernment, of course, requires reflection and critique. I don't care if orgies do work in a culture; the church ought not to sponsor them in place of a turkey supper. Seriously, we must not pitch tent with racist practices, sexist practices, and heterosexist practices.

In our more immediate focus here the church must not pitch tent with the practices of social class. Like those of racism, sexism, and heterosexism, the practices of classism are pervasive in our culture. The purpose of this book is to study the indigenous practices of white working people to discern what their indigenous practices are and how the church may pitch tent with them in order to be a witness to the Word of God in Christ Jesus and to resist, indeed oppose, the systemic practices of social class as they operate in U.S. society.

When I studied social class in college, we typically envisioned a pyramid, or we saw an onion as the shape of the class structure with the wealthy at the top and the poor at the bottom. While such metaphors have utility, it is far more helpful to examine class in terms of social practices. Such an approach makes our efforts much more concrete and serves us well in terms of implications for ministry. Basic to such an approach, of course, is the determination of the practices that are unfaithful and destructive, on the one hand, and those that are basic expressions of the way people engage the world and that offer fruitful residences of God's grace and opportunity for discipleship. Such determinations, of course, need to be careful that our judgments are not themselves classist, and that they are not made unilaterally by middle-class clergy or lay leaders ministering externally with working people.

Parenthetically, I argue for the words *indigenous practices* rather than *contextualization* for two reasons. First, the Enlightenment led elites to believe that they were cosmopolitans and that while primal people had indigenous practices, these elites had universal practices founded in reason and experience. No one has more indigenous practices than so-called cosmopolitans and elites of this kind. Their—our!—privilege, education, and protective insulation make us one of the smallest groups on the face of the earth and profoundly local and parochial. I remember so very well going with a man self-described as "cosmopolitan" and "global" in his thinking to a "trashy" honky tonk. I have never seen anyone so completely unable to engage a situation in my life. Yet, he blamed "them"! All of our lives are located in a history and a culture and a class. We are all local. We are all indigenous.

Second, the word *contextualization* plays into this problem. A subtle bias suggests that those of us with authentic faith must find ways to contextualize that faith in cultures that do not have such genuine expressions. No, this is not true. We are all local people who witness with yet other local people. "We are all beggars telling other beggars where there is bread." Our understanding of the faith is culturally mediated. When we witness to the faith we do so as people within an indigenous culture of our own, proclaiming the truth of Christ to those in yet another indigenous culture. We cannot, we do not, escape this.

The notion of contextualization was first introduced by Shoki Coe of the World Council of Churches. Coe made a distinction between indigenization and contextualization. The former focuses on a response to the gospel in the setting of a traditional culture. The latter, "while not ignoring this, takes into account the process of secularism, technology and the struggle for human justice, which characterizes the historical moment of nations in the Third World." Coe explains that contextualization attempts to understand a culture as ever in a process of change due to influences from within and from without, and not as a static system. My problem with this distinction is that it seems to assume that traditional cultures don't change and that they are not influenced from outside. More than that, it suggests that such cultures have no indigenous concerns about suffering and justice. I sense too much Western presumption in the distinction and in the privileging of the word *contextualization*; that is, I find a stereotyping of traditional culture that sounds too much like the way the West tends to view the other.[2]

The Changing Class Structure

To move more directly into the question of social class it is necessary to make some observations about where we seem to be headed. Fateful and huge forces are at work in this society and around the world along the lines of a growing social inequality. My first step is to name some of these changes.

First, the majority of working-class Americans now is women. One can argue that it has always been so, but only now do we recognize that the work women do at home, for example, is work. But it is also in the working-class jobs outside the home that women now constitute the majority.

Second, the working class is more diverse. Growing numbers of Anglo-European women, racial ethnic men and women, and increases in diversity due to immigration characterize an increasingly complex working class.

Third, class structure is changing as a result of changes in the economy over the past century. In the twentieth century we moved from being a rural society to an urban one. We moved from principally a local to a regional, then to a national and now to a global economy. Our economy has gone from an agricultural to an industrial to a services economy and now increasingly to an informational one.

Fourth, since 1973 a redistribution of income and wealth to the upper end of the class structure resulted in working people receiving a smaller piece of the economic pie. While there has been some closing of the gap between racial ethnic men and women and Anglo-European women in relationship to white working men, this occurred largely because of the losses of the latter, not because all of them have gained.[3]

Fifth, these changes are accompanied by an increasing degradation of work. Working people are working longer and harder with less compensation. What we hear is that the American worker must be better trained if he or she is to benefit from the changes in our economy. This simply is not true. In the U.S. the share of low-skilled workers is decreasing, while the share of low-wage workers is increasing.[4]

A staggering progression of income inequality now characterizes this society. We now pay CEOs millions upon millions of dollars, and wage earners are the losers in that race. Barbara Ehrenreich reports that the Economic Policy Institute found that a "living wage" is $30,000 per year, about $14 per hour. "The shocking thing is that the majority of American workers, about 60 percent, earn less than $14 an hour."[5]

In this connection one other comment is in order. In the last two decades we have heard a good deal to suggest that greed is good and that it works to everyone's benefit. Castell's research counters such claims. His study, on the basis of international research in Western Europe, Asia, the United States, and South America, is that the greedy corporations that fired people, downsized, and retired people who could do the work lost capacity and efficiency. The greedy corporation did not work. Moreover, it is not the hierarchical corporation that does the best work in the emergent economy. Its top-down, and therefore constricted, communication is not adequate to the demands of an information economy. Rather it is the horizontal corporation where people are far more in contact with one another and where there are fewer impediments to flow of communication and information that is the most efficient and effective today. This is the corporate structure best able to function in "the network society."[6] It remains to be seen what impact such corporations will have on working people.

White Working-class People

The focus here will be on white working-class people. Two comments are in order about this focus. First, it is not because I think class factors are unimportant with respect to African Americans, Hispanics/Latinos, Asian Americans, and Native Americans. It is desperately important. Rather, it is because I come out of white working-class America, and I am best able to deal with that. I do not apologize for this focus, but I do want it understood.

Second, I am concerned about how many mainline churches and denominations have lost their capacity to relate to white working-class people. While it is crucial to relate to other racial ethnic groups in this society, my experience is that the church does not address white working-class people in significant ways. So I want to look at working-class whites. Let me say it another way. When you run into an Anglo-European who claims to love other racial ethnic people and claims to be very much attuned to and in touch with women's issues, but does not care about working-class white folks, I get suspicious.

Let me say why. Part of the problem with those of us on the liberal to left wing of the church is that we do not have a lot of material inducement for what we do. There is not a lot of "scratch" for liberals in a helping profession like the ministry. But, if you are on the left of the church, you can get a lot of status and prestige by being "for" certain kinds of things. One of the reasons why some folks hate liberals is that they sense that we care more about our own prestige for being "enlightened" and "progressive" than we care about the issues, and especially the people, on which we have "positions." My hunch is that people who do not care about lower-class whites probably do not care about any kind of people who are poor, except as a kind of "tourist."

One word needs to be said about earthy and profane language. In this book I have used the language of working-class whites, especially as that language occurs in their practices of resistance. I do so for two main reasons. First, earthy and profane language is basic in working-class resistance to establishment or dominant culture. To take out the language or to bleep it is to erase a basic dimension of that resistance, and, in effect, to avoid facing it. In a book on working-class resistance such stratagems will not do. Second, if the church cannot face this language, it will not be able to engage an entire range of tactics of resistance that permeate working-class life. It comes with the territory. At my request Abingdon Press allowed the language to be printed as I had written it. I am grateful, but I alone am responsible for its presence in the book.

To begin a deeper appreciation of the white working class, we need to look at what they are up against. Here we will examine this in terms of the practices of class in the next chapter.

Chapter 2

THE PRACTICES OF CLASS

Perhaps the first step in addressing the issue of class is to see it as a range of practices. What are the practices of social inequality that attend the realities of class? E. P. Thompson's comment in his study on the English working class says that class is not a thing, not a structure, but rather, "Class happens."[1] Class occurs in a range of events that populate our lives. We see it around us all the time. Erving Goffman's notion of rituals of interaction is especially helpful. He argues that society is populated with rituals. For example, if I meet someone, I say, "Hello. How are you?" You say, "I'm fine. How are you?" "What's your name? I'm ——" We go through a ritual of greeting and getting acquainted. In one place Goffman says that society is a wedding, a metaphor he uses to indicate that our social relationships are structured like rituals.[2]

The experience of class, then, can be seen in terms of rituals of inequality. Three such rituals can be named here. The first is the ritual of giving and taking orders. Randall Collins, a sociologist, contends that the study of class can be done, in part, by studying who gives orders and who takes them. He argues that upper-class people mostly give orders and that lower-class people mostly take orders. Middle-class people both give and take orders.[3]

As a former professor in a seminary, I often encountered second-career seminary students. Before they came to seminary some ran their own businesses or were in management positions, or were professionals, and they were the people who basically gave the orders. Then they come to seminary, and suddenly they are students! Not only are they students, but they find out that people who think theologically think "weird," and it takes months, maybe a year, maybe three years, to get to where they can think that way. To move from giving orders to taking them can be a hard experience. But many people live major parts of their lives taking orders. Their lives are populated with rituals of such obedience. Such is the experience and practice of class.

The second ritual of inequality is getting and giving respect. In the realities of class some people receive respect and others must give it. I got a haircut yesterday. I sat down in the chair of a hairdresser near my house and we began to talk.

"My daughter is a hairdresser," I said.

"Oh, really?"

"Yes. How's business out this way?" With that we got into an extended conversation about cutting hair, hairdressing, and the rest. I wanted her to talk about this issue of giving and getting respect. I didn't use that language. But she said,

"You know the worst part of being a hairdresser?"

"No."

She said, "It's the way people treat you. Some people think because you're a hairdresser, you're necessarily dumb. I have people who come here and sit down in my chair, and they think I can't chew gum and walk."

She is quite obviously an intelligent person—it is as plain as day. Then she actually used the line, "They just don't respect you."

The third practice of class is that of deference and demeanor. That is, the practice of class is made up of rituals in which those in the lower reaches of the class structure defer to those at the top of the structure. Such deference also has to do with the very bearing of people, even with their posture in the presence of others. I remember so well working in the oil field with men who were very strong and quite capable. They could do most anything required in terms of maintaining the mechanics and equipment of that field. As we worked in the absence of the bosses, they were confident, typically exuded vitality, and kept a banter of articulate observation and humor going almost interminably. But let the boss of the field come on-site, and suddenly these men were looking at their shoes. Their posture changed, their language changed. The practices of deference and demeanor took over.

Think, then, about a pastor who is in relationships with a host of people in the church and in the community and how that pastor responds to people. Giving orders? Giving respect? What are the patterns of deference and demeanor? It is very easy for a pastor to enter quite actively into such practices of inequality. Our education, our position of "responsibility," the kind of respect we are often accorded in a community: all of these can become occasions for our practice of the rituals of social inequality.

We once invited a person to interview for the presidency of our institution. We were quite positive about him, but we wanted to know how he worked with others on his staff. So the committee sent a few people to interview strategic persons at the candidate's church. They had explicit instructions to talk with the janitor and church secretary who worked with him. We wanted to know how he treated the janitor and how much respect he showed to the secretary. In this case, I'm delighted to say that he came through with flying colors. But it is a test we need to use more often in the church as a means of making us sensitive to issues of class. If such became standard practice, it would influence the way professionals relate to people they work with.

The Politics of Distinction

Closely related to the practices of class is another range of practices I call the politics of distinction and the strategies of condescension. How do people attain distinction? How do people express it? How does the issue of class manifest itself in a politics of this kind?

The Use of Language

Basic to the politics of distinction is the use of language. It can be enormously subtle or as overt as a sledgehammer. I remember taking my pickup to trade it in on a new one, so I went to this agency to make a deal. The salesperson asks me what I do for a living. When I tell him I am a professor, he asks:

"Mr. Sample, why do you want a pickup?"

"Well, I believe on the basis of my tradition that pickups are more beautiful than automobiles." He is unimpressed with that and offers an alternative view:

"Mr. Sample, could I suggest to you that while a pickup is perhaps practical, you need a vehicle that will reflect your position and financial maturity?"

He wants to sell me a car that will cost a lot more, of course, but note what he has just done to me with language. He tells me that my love of pickups is extrinsic and utilitarian (practical), not intrinsic and substantive. More than that, he suggests that my taste is inappropriate and needs to be consonant with my "position." And perhaps even worse, he has declared that my taste is developmentally delayed (not in keeping with my "financial maturity"). In doing it, he is attempting to undermine my taste in pickups!

Note the polarities of language he employs and implies. Such binary use of language is pervasive in the realities of class. We say people have "class" and "no class." We talk about people who are "distinguished" and those who are "trash." I think especially of the use of "highbrow" and "lowbrow" in discussing taste in music and the arts. The emergence of this distinction is interesting. It comes from so-called scientists who studied phrenology (heads) and physiognomy (faces). They decided that people who were intelligent, who

had culture, who had learning, possessed high fore-
heads ("highbrow") but the people who were low in
intelligence, lacking in character, morality, and learning, they were "lowbrow." Interestingly enough, the
scientists tended to look like the highbrow types. The
"lowbrows" were people of other racial ethnic groups.
This is an outright racist, bipolar use of language. Yet,
it has entered our commonplace language.[4]

The Conspiracy of Taste

Closely related to such use of language is a politics
of class in terms of the conspiracy of taste. I think particularly here of the way in which one canon of taste
can be used to castigate another canon of taste and
with it the people who hold such tastes. No music
more graphically and more narratively expresses the
lives of white working-class Americans in the United
States than country music. As with any genre of music
it needs and deserves critique, yet I am continually
amazed at the cavalier dismissal of such music by so-
called progressives who describe it as nasal and twangy
"tear in my beer" music. They would not attack the
blues and jazz music of African Americans because
they know good and well that they would be taken on
in a devastating and rightful attack for their racist
views. Yet, I dare say that the criteria for assessing jazz
and blues are not dissimilar from those of country
music in terms of the fact that such criteria are drawn
from the tradition of the genre itself. To attack jazz
and blues would mean the critics are not progressive.
Or notice the "cosmopolitan" claims made by so many

progressives about Native American music, which certainly would not normally meet the implicit criteria of such "global thinkers," but again notice the frequent testimonies of appreciation for it. The point here is not that one must like every genre of music, but rather if one wants to take sides with people who are marginal—a concept that can be insufferable in the patronizing way it can be and often is used—then surely a greater attempt to get in touch with the soul music—the music with which people are encoded and which tells their story—is required. I have argued in another context that classical music is used in the United States to legitimate social inequality. While I make no case that such is intrinsic to classical music, it is so used.[5]

The work of Paul DiMaggio demonstrates how classical music in the nineteenth century removed itself increasingly from events of more popular appeal to instantiate itself with the elites of this society. Early in the nineteenth century in Boston the arts were engaged in a wide mix of levels, types, and styles, and a broad cross section of people from the upper, middle, and working classes participated in them. Dimaggio reports that "Museums were modeled on Barnum's" and that "fine art was interspersed among such curiosities as bearded women and mutant animals."[6] Yet, by the end of the century, sharp class divisions had been made between "high" and "low" culture and the legitimation of social inequality was well underway.

Lawrence Levine also observes the role of the arts in issues of class. He demonstrates how cultural categories are constructed in order to make social inequalities appear "natural" and thereby deny the creative and artistic endeavors of an entire social class in wholesale fashion. Social class and certain non-white racial ethnic groups are construed in the lower end of this hierarchy and accorded primitive status.[7]

Robert Walser sees this same kind of racism and classism as still quite present. "People are constantly being typed by their cultural allegiances, respected or dismissed because of the music they like." He observes that what is worse is that people begin to believe these demeaning characterizations of their traditions and their lives. Walser concludes that "cultural hierarchy functions to naturalize social hierarchies through the circular reinscription of prestige."[8] As a matter of fact, we often do not realize how historically and socially located (including class) our constructions of taste are.

Much of the tradition of classical music and the "higher arts" are informed by the notion of art for art's sake. I believe it also influences our worship styles. This construction receives its most classic formulation in the third critique of Immanuel Kant where he discusses his aesthetics. He argues there that the aesthetic gaze is a pure one, that is, that art is enjoyed purely for itself: art for the sake of art alone. It has no utilitarian purpose. Kant describes such aesthetic enjoyment as "purposeless purposefulness." Such aesthetic pleasure is detached, indifferent, disinterested, and distanced.[9]

Such claims need analysis from the standpoint of class. Back in the 1960s my wife, Peggy, and I had good friends in the Boston area I shall call "Joe" and "Mary." These are fictitious names for real people. Joe came out of a very wealthy family and Mary from a well-to-do one. Both of them were deeply involved in the civil rights movement in the 60s and actively opposed the Vietnam War. They put their money and their lives into these issues. They had that kind of courage and commitment. We enjoyed both of them and became close friends. I remember one evening we went to *La Boheme* in Boston. That's probably my favorite of all the operas.

The scene I especially love is when Mimi comes down to get a light from Rodolfo, whom she does not know. They are bohemians living in this tenement and quite poor. Mimi's candle has gone out and she knocks on Rodolpho's door to have it relit. In the course of their introduction, Rodolpho, accidentally-on-purpose, extinguishes his own light so as to make a play for Mimi. With both of them searching on the floor for her keys, which Mimi has dropped, Rodolpho moves over toward her and putting his hand on hers begins the beautiful aria, "Che gelida manina" ("What a frozen little hand"). He tells her that he is a poet and that he makes his living squandering "rhymes and love songs like a lord." In response Mimi sings "Mi Chiamano Mimi" ("They call me Mimi"). She then tells him that she sews flowers on linen. "It's my pleasure to make roses and lilies. I love those things which possess such sweet enchantment." Back to back, here we have two of Puccini's best arias. Their meeting is then interrupted by Rodolpho's friends inviting him to the pub. Rodolpho responds to them and then he and Mimi move into this "conversation" about their emerging love for one another. I think this long section of the two arias and the "conversation" is some of the most rapturous music in the Western world. This scene ends when Mimi and Rodolfo express their love for each other. They sing/shout (the way opera singers can sing and communicate a shout without losing vocal and musical control), "Ah amor, amor, amor!"[10]

On the first "Amor" both tenor and soprano are at the top of the staff. And in the theater that night, it is so beautiful that I can hardly stand it. I am a classical music Pentecostal. I am unconsciously miming the conductor. I am moving and going through spasms with the turns of the music. Peggy elbows me and says, "You are shaking the whole row!" As they move further upscale and go to the second "Amor" I think I cannot stand it. My gyrations increase. On the third "Amor" the soprano is in the stratosphere, the tenor just beneath her. I am in heart-bursting ecstasy. As the scene ends I am emotionally a line of wrung-out, washed clothes hanging in a windstorm of musical power. I leap from my chair, shouting bravo, jumping up and down and applauding to my loud whistles and top-of-the-lungs screams of "All right! Yes! Yes! Yes!!!"

I look at Joe. While standing, he is doing this patter with his hands, a soft clapping that made me think he was at a different event. His demeanor is calm. One could say disinterested, detached, distanced, and indifferent.

"Joe, didn't you like it?" I ask.

"I thought it was extremely well done."

"*Did you really like it?*" I asked again because his response was emotionally flat, really more like the repose of death.

"Oh, I thought the voice control and the blend of the soprano and tenor were exquisitely done. The last progressions were especially effective. It was a superlative performance." He said all of this with a kind of clinical dispatch, the way a big city coroner might describe a cadaver after a long holiday weekend.

"Uh huh," was my concluding but unconvinced response.

That night Peggy and I were brushing our teeth, getting ready to go to sleep, and I said, "Honey, I feel sorry for Mary."

"What?"

"I feel sorry for Mary."

"What are you talking about?"

"I'd hate to make love to Joe."

"What on earth are you talking about?"

"If he ever moved, she'd think she hurt him."

This story illustrates two different constructions of taste. Joe's, of course, is quite Kantian. His own education in private schools and in an Ivy League university, his socialization in his family and their upper-class association, and his own style are quite clearly part of the Kantian historical construction. For him, aesthetic pleasure is pleasure of a subjective kind that seeks to be derived purely from art itself that is not employed to engender emotional responses such as the one I displayed at the opera. Kant says, "Taste that requires an added element of charm and emotion for its delight, not to speak of adopting this as a measure of its approval, has not emerged from barbarism."[11]

But I come out of a different construction. The best way to name it is to take phrases from two country music songs. The first comes from the song "Redneck, White Socks and Blue Ribbon Beer." The song lyrics say, "No, we don't fit in with that white-collar crowd, we're a little too rowdy and a little too loud." The other phrase comes from Mary Chapin Carpenter's "Down at the Twist and Shout." I combine these with the phrase "rowdy and loud at the Twist and Shout." The Kantian and the working-class constructions of taste are almost polar opposites of each other.[12]

It does not take much imagination to see what happens to a pastor or other religious leader who comes out of the Kantian tradition of taste and takes up life with a working-class congregation whose construction of taste is more of the "rowdy and loud at the Twist and Shout" tradition. It would be far too easy for the pastor, say, to be seen as like the boss, or like the "snobs" working people know only too well. And it is a mistake to believe that such things are not perceived by working people.

More than that, such perceptions are simply part of the popular culture. In the musical comedy *Carousel*, by Richard Rogers and Oscar Hammerstein II, the male lead, Billy Bigelow, upon learning that his new love, Julie, is pregnant with their child, sings his "Soliloquy" in anticipation of his romanticized "son" who turns out later to be a she. But in describing his future unborn son he sings that he never wants his son to marry the boss's snobby daughter "who'll give him a peck and call it a kiss and look in his eyes through a lorgnette." Notice the flat, passionless affect of the boss's daughter. The emotional cool of elites is not lost on working people.[13]

I remember working in the oil field that when the gang members wanted to mock and disdain a boss who was quite straight in manner and no little fastidious, they would walk around in this casual, withdrawn, unengaged stroll and then loudly shout out amid roars of laughter that "he made love with a wet washrag in his hand." This latter comment is meant to suggest that his affect was so controlled and his style so tidy that his preoccupation with order and neatness, and his lack of emotion kept him from ever being truly engaged in an act even as erotic as intercourse!

There is in all of this an implicit knowing of the politics of distinction and the role of taste and resistance to it. Working with the thought of Mikhail Bakhtin the sociologist, Pierre Bourdieu observes:

> The popular imagination can only invert the relationship which is the basis of the aesthetic sociodicy: responding to sublimation by a strategy of reduction or degradation, as in slang, parody, burlesque or caricature, using obscenity or scatology to turn arsy-versy, head over heels, all the "values" in which the dominant groups project and recognize their sublimity, it rides roughshod over difference, flouts distinction, and like the Carnival games, reduces the distinctive pleasures of the soul to the common satisfactions of food and sex.[14]

My major difference with Bourdieu is that he does not develop the constructive and quite positive dimensions of working-class taste. It is perhaps telling about his own view that he seems to see working-class taste as too much derivative of, resistant to, and dependent on elitist fashions. The constructive task is yet to be done.

The Imposition of Practices

A final dimension of the politics of distinction we can consider in this space is that of the imposition of practices from one social location, typically privileged, onto working-class people. This is a complex area and one that can only be touched on briefly.

Continuing some of the comments made above about the use of binary opposites in language in the practices of class, a further word can be said about the imperialism of language in the politics of distinction. One basic expression of this is the colonial use of categories, especially from pop psychology, to characterize working-class lives. Such categories abound in professional work in this society and no little of it in ministry. Notice the use of terms like *dysfunctionality* and *codependence* and the ways these are thrown around and employed to characterize working-class people. When I hear those words used by a professional person about working people, I want to know how they arrived at such conclusions.

You will forgive my impertinence if I suggest that these pop psychologists often lack much grounding in the discipline of psychology and even less in social and political training. Basic to the captivity of class is the freedom that people in the helping professions seem to have to lasso people of lower classes in imperialistic categories imposed externally and in psychological stereotyping that obscures the struggles of working people and dismisses the lived concrete reality of their lives. To be clear, I do not mean that terms like *dysfunctional* and *codependence* cannot be used carefully to describe behavior damaging to working-class people. What I often see, however, is a use of such language out of touch with the solidarity of working-class life, a use that betrays the individualism and careerism of professional striving.

A second expression of the politics of distinction is the imposition of linguistic practices coming out of middle-class business and professional life. I think, for example, of the imposition of the discursive practices of those trained in literate, academic circles, that is, those trained in the use of a discourse, meaning here the language that grows out of a specialization or discipline. The problem is that most working people are more oral than literate. While they can read and write, at least most of them, they engage the world through proverbs, stories, and thinking in terms of people they know rather than philosophers and theologians they have read.

The professional and managerial classes are noted for their use of introspective practices and an ongoing focus on their own interiority. While working-class people are not without self-insight and concern about their inward states, nevertheless they are not typically occupied with their "innards" on the scale of the middle class. I think here of the pastor who is "into"

Myers-Briggs and other aspects of the "world religion" of Carl Jung and Joseph Campbell, and I flinch with pain at the thought of him or her being unleashed on a working-class congregation. I remember so well a working-class woman who had given up on going to worship in her church and restricted her participation to her Sunday school class because her pastor, she said, "thinks he's a shrink."

Or, I worry about those who bring their organizational practices out of the modern corporation or the university. Such practices are powerfully goal-oriented with a profound utilitarian bent. They stress "vision" and that with a highly conceptual and theoretical flair born of higher education. Working people are not nearly so goal-oriented as they are "gather-oriented." The basic practice of effective working-class congregations is the gathering. Board meetings are more like a gathering than like an organization. Meetings are more like gatherings than they are like committees. A Sunday school class will look a lot more like a gathering than like a classroom of instruction. Now, a great deal can be done at a gathering. Much can happen at such events, but the practice is significantly different from the organizational format of most bureaucratic approaches. The gathering is even more effective than the acclaimed nonhierarchical "network" of contemporary organizational life. This is not to say such practices don't need critique, certainly they do, but it will be a critique that grows out of working-class life, not one based in the analyses and conceptualities of highly literate work of text-based practices.

The most effective pastors are those who honor the practices of working-class life and who join those practices. In the incarnational sense, they "pitch tent." Pastors who pitch tent convey a love of working-class people that is difficult to convey on that scale in any other way. It registers not only that one understands the people; it witnesses to a respect and ultimately a love of who they are and, maybe even more important on some days, what they are up against.

I do understand that a pastor or lay leader can take on too much of a with-it style in attempting to pitch tent. Such efforts often look awkwardly overdone or maybe just plain silly. In instances like these it is better simply to confess one's lack of experience or skill, and at that point simply ask to be taught.

Let me draw this section to a close with a summary comment. If we are to engage in indigenous ministry with working-class white people, we need to understand the practices of class and the ways that their lives are populated with rituals of social inequality. In theological language these practices are principalities and powers. The concrete, lived practices of taking orders, of giving and often not getting respect, of demeaning insults to one's dignity, of the heavily sanctioned deference expected from working people, which is systemic—these are the required litanies of the liturgies of class. Working-class white people understand all too well the politics of distinction, and, while they may not name those as we have here, their implicit knowing of such things grows from an inhabited residence in the structures and happenings of class.

It would be strange indeed if working people did not resist these practices of class and this captivity. These are flesh and blood people, and they do find ways to resist the domination and discounting they experience. To fail to see such resistance as a politics is to lose a central opportunity for ministry. We turn to this next.

Chapter 3

THE PRACTICES OF RESISTANCE

The realities of class are the occasion for a politics of everyday resistance on the part of working people. Identifying this politics and learning to work with it are basic to ministry with working-class people. In stressing everyday resistance I am distinguishing it from a more overt political resistance, such as organizing around candidates, union organizing, or various social issues or community organizing, to name just a few examples. John Fisk argues that everyday resistance takes place in terms of a different range of meanings, pleasures, and identities.[1] These are often enacted "under the noses of the dominant culture." In other words, they may look simply like the environment, but much challenge is afoot.

One of the forms that everyday resistance takes with working people is in their refusal of the dominant discourse. For example, they refuse fancy talk and will refuse to use correct English, especially if they know it is expected. Such resistance can also make a pointed use of four-letter words.[2] I was walking down the street in my community a few years ago. About a hundred yards away, I see a woman who is a friend of mine. She is talking to four guys standing there in the middle of the street. They all know I'm clergy, and, when I get within hearing distance, she says, "Hey, Tex, how the fuck are ya?" Well, these guys don't know me well, and they immediately enter into this ritual of looking at their feet, and I can just "hear" them saying to themselves, "Oh, my God, what has she done?" They do not know what to do. It just completely stops them. Knowing her as I do, my grasp of her action is simply that she knows I am a preacher, but she is not going to let my presence affect the way she acts. She is not going to change the way she relates to people just because I walk up. I am aware that she likes me a good deal, but she is not going to change who she is just because a member of the cloth happens to come on the scene. It does not have to do with me personally; it has to do with her being true to herself and to her resistance to the dominant etiquette with respect to the clergy. She rejects that. Such is one instance of everyday resistance.

A politics of resistance often takes the form of a refusal to overdo it, which is a refusal of propriety, of doing what is proper.[3] The dominant etiquette is a basic part of the problem of class for many working people. It is simply one more way that the politics of distinction gets carried out. Our son, Steve, was an alcoholic. He actively abused alcohol for some fourteen years. He achieved sobriety through the help of an AA biker gang. They were crucial to his recovery. After joining that gang he never used alcohol or any other drug again. Later, when he was accidentally killed on his motorcycle, one of the first people to come to the wake was a man named Reverend Joe. So help me, this guy weighs 300 pounds and he has on a vest but no shirt. And he has hair on his chest, back, and shoulders thicker than most people have on their heads. He comes to the wake and says to the funeral director at the door of the chapel, "I've come to see Steve's body, I'm Reverend Joe."

Notice, this man is not going to change his attire, especially for the wake of a friend. In fact, his attire and his style are, in part, the way he "shoves it up the nose"—or some other aperture—of the dominant society. Resisting the dominant code, resisting established etiquette, taste, affect, is just basic to everyday resistance.

Think with me about a honky-tonk for a minute. When you go into one, at least when I do, I am overwhelmed by the cigarette smoke. You can cut it with a knife. You say to yourself, "Why in the world don't they do something about the cigarette smoke?" The answer to that question is easy: Because they don't want anyone there who has problems with it. Basic to the draw of a honky-tonk is the fact that it is not a place where the people of the dominant society go. It is perhaps the central institution of everyday resistance.

Yet another form that resistance takes is to set up spaces in the places of the powerful. I draw this point from Michel de Certeau. He states that the powerful set up places, large buildings and open areas. The powerless, then, set up spaces in the midst of the places of power in order to live and to resist. Power builds places, the powerless set up spaces in the midst of the places.[4]

I was working in South Carolina several years ago. We were focusing on the old mill churches of that area and what had happened to them. During my presentation I introduced de Certeau's notion of resistance as setting up spaces in the places of the powerful. On a break, one of the pastors comes over and says, "Tex, I have got to tell you about my dad because he is a perfect illustration of setting up a space in the midst of the places of the powerful. My dad was a farmer during the Depression and he lost the farm. He simply couldn't sustain it. So he had to go to work at the mill. We lived in a mill house on mill land, bought from the mill store, and my dad went to work in the mill every day. When spring came, he took a shovel, a hoe, and a rake and dug a garden in one corner of that yard. He went into that garden before he went to work at the mill. When the mill day was over, he'd come home, and he would work that garden every evening. You know what my dad was doing? He was saying to the world, 'I am a farmer, and I'm always going to be a farmer, and by God, I'm gonna farm this plot of land even if I do have to work in that mill.' My dad resisted what happened to him all his life." I think that's dead right.

William A. Wilson tells the story of Mormon women when polygamy was still practiced by that tradition. One of these women told the story of the day that her husband came home to tell her why he had to take a second wife. With her sitting in his lap he begins to go through the reasons for his decision. As he tells her, she urinates all over both of them. In other instances the married Morman women would empty chamber pots on the marital beds of the newlyweds of a polygamous relationship. That's resistance![5]

What does that have to do with ministry? Two comments are in order. First, the worst thing a pastor can do is to get in a spot where he or she fights against such resistance. To do so is to join the dominant culture. It is to become part of the problem as understood by working people.

Second, the best thing a pastor can do in terms of these issues is to find the spaces of resistance and to join the people in them. My suspicion is that few points in working life have the energy and passion invested in such spaces of resistance. So look for these expressions of resistance and join them. Many of the so-called apathetic congregations of working people are more likely to be locations of congealed anger. To search for the places where everyday resistance is lived out is to find the spaces of deep motivation and yearning. Basic to such work is the recognition of everyday resistance.

James C. Scott studied peasants and arrived at a host of forms that their resistance takes. His list serves very well for examining the forms resistance takes in many congregations and local communities among the working class. Such people know how to sap the strength of external forces through foot dragging, sabotage, false compliance, noncompliance, feigned ignorance, slander, and gossip. Resistance like this works through low-profile techniques that usually require little or no planning or coordination, and all of these can be carried out through informal networks with implicit under-standings. Typically, this kind of resistance avoids direct confrontation with authority. It is so very effec-tive because it can nibble policies to death and sustain itself triumphantly over the long haul. No pastor, no church leader wants to be the object of this kind of resistance, but I am afraid it occurs in no few situations where there is not a commitment to pitch tent with the resistance of working people.[6]

In this connection, the work of Mikhail Bakhtin is quite helpful as well. He studied working people in the Middle Ages. Yet, his findings are quite current. He describes how the lower classes used festivals and car-nivals to express resistance. Such events could make "possible and . . . justify the most extreme freedom and frankness of thought and speech." These events were occasion to cancel hierarchies, and expose and undo pretense. Mockery, derision, and debasement were basic to their work. These classes had a deep suspicion of "official truth" and of "the official world." In those times the working people would hold side-street skits in which they would uncrown the king! Bakhtin calls them "side-street displays without footlights." Such resistance represented a complete exit from the present order of this life.[7]

These forms of resistance are not dead, especially in their capacity for mockery and debasement. I have a friend named Dewain who is a heating and cooling man. He basically does duct work for homes and build-ings. He was at my house one day and "got started" on a well-known televangelist who has experienced no little trouble. Dewain began to tell stories about the man. Speaking in a high-pitched voice and spitting out his barrage in a rapid-fire approach, he would splice one story about the televangelist with some kind of "proverb" about "not getting caught with your hand in the chicken coop." He moved with remarkable agility from story to proverb and back again. It was just a superb display. Finally he comes to his punch line: "Tex, you know what? That guy could count his balls twice and come up with a different number both times."

Let me clarify here. Dewain is not talking about the televangelist's capacity to count, he is talking about the fact that he's out of touch with the world. In theological language, he's lost. The mockery, the travesty, the derision, the debasement were all there, not to mention the festive way in which he engaged in his own side-street performance without footlights!

Traditional Politics

Let us move now to yet another issue in terms of resistance. It has to do with a discussion of the politics of working-class people. Where are they politically? The first answer, and it would be correct, is that they are quite diverse. But I want to search for a dominate mode, certainly not the whole picture, perhaps not even the majority, although I think it is. This may vary with younger working adults; I don't have enough data on them—more about them later.

Though the more careful studies find that working people tend to be more moderate than liberal or conservative, I think that they are not really right, left, or middle. That continuum is basically a modern one, and most working people do not really fit it. Rather, most working people are committed to a traditional politics. By "traditional" I do not mean "conservative." Rebecca Klatch has distinguished sharply between traditional and conservative political views. In her study of Christian Right women she argues that a conservative believes in:

1. The free individual
2. Competition
3. The free market
4. The minimalist state
5. High military spending
6. Pursuit of self-interest
7. Biggest fear: the erosion of liberty

A traditionalist politics—which she calls a sociomoral conservative, in contrast, holds to:

1. The centrality of the family
2. Seeing the world through a religious lens
3. Cooperation
4. Commitment to basic institutions like the family, the school, and the church
5. Respectability and moral living
6. Greatest fear: moral decay[8]

In other words it is the difference between those who are laissez-faire economic conservatives and those who are socio-moral traditionalists. One example can sharpen the difference. A conservative stresses the free individual. No true traditionalist is going to defend that! James Ault Jr. in his study of a Jerry Falwell church found that most of the people there were socio-moral traditionalists more than they were laissez-faire conservatives. Basic to his findings is that traditionalism is a means for controlling male sociality. That is, the man is the one who has had the marketable skills in the family throughout most of our history in the U.S. If he should pursue his self-interest, he may go out the door to chase his own dreams or, as it often happens, to pursue the other woman. Ault contends that traditionalism attempts to prevent this with its commitments to family, to basic institutions, and to morality.[9]

Listen in this regard to an important country music song: "Mamas, don't let your babies grow up to be cowboys," which then suggests the would-be cowboys should be doctors or lawyers instead. You may question such confidence in doctors and lawyers. "They tryst around, they leave, they walk out the door," you say. Yes, but you can sue the hell out of 'em, and get something for it. But also note the fear in another part of the lyrics of the song: "Cowboys ain't easy to love and they're harder to hold."[10] There is the issue in the traditionalist attempt to establish order in the ever-present potential for chaos in working-class life. Many working-class families are a paycheck away from poverty, and the man's paycheck is typically the larger of the two in a two-income family. There's a radical difference between this kind of traditionalist politics, on the one hand, and laissez-faire conservative politics, on the other. The function of the latter is to advance the interests of the privileged. The former attempts to barricade against a world where most working people never get ahead and where the threat of disaster is ever there.

Populist Anarchism

Another dimension of resistance is pervasive in working-class life and it is often misunderstood. I contend that the largest group of working people in the U.S. is committed to a populist anarchism. In using the language of anarchism I do not mean classical anarchism as with a thinker like Peter A. Kropotkin, and I certainly do not mean to convey the popular image of anarchism that sees desperate cartoon figures running around with bombs in their hands. I decidedly do not have in view people who blow up government buildings in Oklahoma City. This latter instance is serious and requires attention, but such acts are the work of a lunatic fringe. But this is not, of course, where most working people are by any means. Obviously, too, I do not mean acts of terrorism of more recent history.

Populist anarchism is a response to the constraints of the realities of class. It grows from this larger set of practices of resistance we have examined. It takes form with people who want to be "free from the institutional entrapments of the modern world."[11] Not political in the programmatic sense, it proposes no set of priorities for the nation and hence is not ideological in the sense that it has an explicit position on social policy. Rather, it is highly suspicious of social control and the formal, legal ways of the dominant culture. It distrusts theory and theorists, and fine print and "fancy talk" are subjected to constant suspicion. While there is a deep love of country, it is accompanied by a commensurate distrust of government. In many cases it amounts to wanting to be left the hell alone.

A former student tells the story of an acquaintance of his who worked in a factory outside Des Moines. This man lived in a house outside the city limits. He moved out there because he was sick and tired of people always telling him what to do. One year the county decided to run a water line through his yard, for which the city had eminent domain. While the man thought his area needed a new water main, no one bothered to ask him before they began to dig across the back of his yard. He would have gladly given permission, but they did not ask. He comes home one day, and there is this ditch across his backyard. What's more they leave the ditch-digging and earth-moving equipment in his sizable backyard, again without asking. He just goes into the house, gets a 12-gauge shotgun, loads it, comes out and blows out every window in that digger and the earth-moving machine. He said later: "If the sons of bitches would've asked me, I'd have been glad to let 'em. I would have helped 'em dig the goddam ditch, but they didn't even ask me. So I shot the fuckin' windows out of their fuckin' machines." When the case went to court—to the judge's credit—he said to the company, "He's right. Leave him alone. Next time you do something like that, ask." The man got off free!

If one thinks that such populist anarchism is strictly a male stance and activity, let me beg to differ. I shall never forget my grandmother, who was not political in the sense of national or even local politics. Politics was not really a part of her life, unless it intruded into the lives of her family or friends. The chief of police once slapped my uncle, her son-in-law, because he would not give the chief more money to look the other way while he sold whiskey unlawfully on Main Street. My grandmother opposed her son-in-law's bootlegging. She was a devoted Christian who hated whiskey. She also opposed the chief being on the take, but when she heard that the chief had slapped a member of her family rather than arrest him, she called the chief on the phone and told him in no uncertain words, "If you ever slap my son-in-law or anyone else in my family ever again, I am going to bring my broom to town and whip your ass up and down both sides of Main Street!"

The chief never again slapped, or, so far as I know, even had a face-to-face encounter with anyone in the family. The image of an old woman acting out her populist anarchism and beating his posterior up and down the major thoroughfare of our town must have been a scene to avoid at all costs.

As delightful as the two examples above are, let me also say that a populist anarchism can take racist and bigoted forms. The militia movement in the U.S. is an example, though an extremist one, and certainly does not represent where the overwhelming mass of working people are. Yet, we ought not be complacent about it. At exactly this point, however, we need to address issues of racial justice and those of class together. When this happens, a very powerful coalition can come into being. I remember when Jesse Jackson went into Iowa to address the farm crisis there. He spent days—weeks, I recall—visiting with farmers and working people in Iowa, talking about their problems and concerns. He took an active interest in their lives. Farmers and workers had been an ongoing issue for him for some time. After Jackson's visits in Iowa I spent a long afternoon with a farmer who was losing his farm during that crisis. I shall never forget that when Jesse Jackson's name came up, the man spoke with the utmost respect and appreciation for Jackson. We need much more of that kind of working across lines of class and race.

Family versus Career

One other dimension of working-class life that connects actively with everyday resistance is the role of extended family. I referred to James Ault's work above. In his study of a Jerry Falwell Fundamentalist Baptist Church outside Worcester, Massachusetts, he names a basic difference between the working people he found there and college-trained managers and professionals like himself. He found that working people lived "lives organized in circles of cooperating kin" or in organizations or relationships like these.[12] In these circles, practices of reciprocity are the norm for people who could not get by without helping each other out. I remember a friend of mine, a Teamster, who in his spare time replaced the entire engine of my Plymouth with that of his junk Dodge that still had a usable engine. When he finished—it ran well—I asked him what I owed him. His response was, "What's the matter with you? What do you think friends are for?" It is easy to forget how much working-class people depend on the giving and receiving of favors and how important this is in their coping and survival.

Basic to professional lives, Ault reports, is the necessity to leave home and with it family dependencies. Professionals become "self-governing individuals" who are free to move from one place to another first in pursuit of higher education and then in career ladder moves. The educated professional has to "piece together a meaningful life with new friends and colleagues alongside old ones." Meanwhile, one's material well-being does not depend on "a stream of daily reciprocities within a family-based circle of people known in common." Instead the necessities of life are met by career promotions with salary increases and good benefits.[13]

As one can imagine, this difference in social location can lead to no little working-class resistance to professional people and their vaunted lives. One illustration of this will have to do in this space, that of morality. In the world of those at the Falwell church, biblically based morality was understood in absolutes. It was "fixed and transcendent," says Ault. These socio-moral traditionalists, for example, stated firmly that "divorce is wrong" and "God is against it." Yet, there were divorced people in the congregation. What Ault found was an upholding of the absolutes, on the one hand, and a flexibility and adaptability in using those absolutes, on the other. In one instance a woman had an affair with a man at work and left her husband, a nephew of one of the church's deacons. Nevertheless the church approved her divorce from the man because he had neglected his family's needs by getting drunk, smoking pot, riding his snow-mobile, and having "a great time." He was considered lazy and an unfaithful provider who left his wife vulnerable to an affair.

What's going on here? The organic character of a close-knit community based on face-to-face relationships is sustained by the biblical teachings as absolutes. They are not mere window dressing but are basic to a moral order that sustains these networks of cooperating kin. These absolutes, moreover, attempt to "combat the tide of moral relativism and individualism they object to in the culture around them."[14] In this sense these moral absolutes take an active form of resistance to the wider culture, especially that of the "situational ethics" of professional and managerial groups.

At the same time, these absolutes are used with more flexibility not in "any explicit qualification but, instead, in the occasions of their actual use, guided firmly yet tacitly by a collective sense of the particularities of so many situations at hand." As a result these fundamentalists can "accommodate the growing incidence of divorce in American life, for instance, without abandoning their general prohibition of it."[15]

Let me say, this use of moral absolutes in sometimes flexible and supple ways is not hypocrisy. It is the claiming of moral commitment in a world of relativism that nevertheless faces into the fact that people violate these absolutes in ways that destroy the relationships they are meant to sustain. But you do not build a moral order by beginning with these more specific exceptions that arise.

In the dictionary language of the educated classes, an absolute is an absolute and permits no exceptions. In the moral order of these fundamentalist working people, an absolute is a commitment to the Bible and to relationships of extended kin. Its exceptions are not the foundations of a quandary ethics, but a tacit acknowledgment that an absolute cannot work where the relationships no longer hold. This is not the situational ethics of professional and managerial careerists who are seen by working people as trying to rationalize their way out of basic commitments to family and faith. Managerial/professional talk of choices, of self-fulfilling autonomy, and the balancing out of conflicting moral claims seems to working people like no more than ducking responsibility and one's duty to family.

Furthermore, absolutes are a way to get in the face of and stick up the [apertures] of managerial/professional classes. Commitment to a different moral order is itself a form of resistance and an important one. It not only grows out of the extended relationship of their lives and helps sustain those relationships but also it provides a sense of moral superiority, albeit one that at times seems too compensative.

Let me be clear; Ault's study is of a fundamentalist church. I am not suggesting that all working people see morality the way this Falwell Baptist Church does. Most working people are not fundamentalists. In another book I have described working-class respectables who are similar in their approach to morality to those in Ault's church, not so much in a fundamentalist commitment to the Bible, but in the sense of a traditionalist approach to conventional morality significantly tied to extended family life. Such a morality functions much like that of the people in Ault's study.[16]

Yet, not all working people are like these either. My study of hard-living working-class people demonstrated a different morality than that of the Falwell church or of working-class respectables. I defined hard-living people as those characterized by uneven employment histories, alcohol and other drug abuse, unstable marital relationships, and records of household violence as abusers or victims or both. These are hardly biblical or conventional! At the same time, it is interesting that when hard-living people talk of changing their ways and of getting their lives straightened out, the image of what they considered a good life looked a great deal like that of this conventional kind, if not a biblical one.[17]

But let the final word here be that many working people come out of a social location of extended family ties that typically stands in sharp contrast to the career trajectories of business and professional life. This social location is accompanied by a morality at odds with the situational ethics of the free autonomous individualism of middle-class achievement striving. This gap is the source of no little resistance by the working class, a fact that ought not be ignored in an understanding of the everyday resistance of their lives.

This chapter suggests how pervasive everyday resistance is in working-class life: in rejection of the practices of class, in traditional politics, in populist anarchism, and in traditional morality. We need now to begin a turn toward doing ministry in a context of working-class resistance by examining the practices of religious faith and devotion. We go here in the next chapter.

Chapter 4

FAITH COMMITMENT OF THE HEART

O ne day Shucks Burt and I were laying a pipeline through a swamp. (In the oil field you always lay pipeline through swamp, and you always lay them in ten inches of water. The reason you do so is because you wear eight-inch boots.) This job requires us to go to the big pipe rack and load a truck with two-hundred-pound joints of pipe, twenty feet long, and then take them to the edge of a swamp. From there we must hand-carry them out across that swamp laying them end to end. After they are laid out, you then come back and "make them up" (which means screw them together). After loading the truck we drove to the side of the swamp and got out of the truck. Standing beside the trailer Shucks says, "Hey, college boy, you get up there on the front end of that pipe and lead out across the swamp."

I say, "Well, OK, but why do you want me to lead?"

"Hell, I ain't going to have some college boy drop a pipe behind me and kill me. You get up there. I want you where I can see you."

I said, "Well, what if you drop the pipe?"

"It'd be a good loss, college boy. Besides, there's water moccasins out there. You don't think I'm going to go first, do you?"

I'm scared to death of a cottonmouth water moccasin. They are aggressive snakes. They will come after you. They are fearsome creatures. But there is nothing to do but grab that pipe and head out across that swamp. As we slosh out through the mud and water, Shucks starts in again, "Hey, college boy, what do you believe about the virgin birth?" He often asked such questions out of the blue. He loved to trap people, especially me, so I was not surprised by a question, only by *this* question. But I had had a course on Introduction to Philosophy of Religion, I'd had another on the History of Christianity, and yet another on Religious Ethics. I had heady academic status as a wise fool.

I said, "Well, Shucks, you've got to look at the context of that culture and you've got to look at the differences in the language used in the Old Testament and compare it with the language in the New Testament, and you've got to ask what it means to be both divine and human." That's about as far I got. He breaks in, "College boy, I didn't ask you what you thought; I asked you what you believe!"

Believing and Feeling

It took me some twenty years to understand what was going on with Shucks that day. I would later realize that, while I was into training in higher education that privileged thinking and knowing the faith, Shucks approached faith, like most working people, in terms of believing and feeling. For him thinking and knowing seemed to have too much of an indecisive quality about them, an entertainment of options that avoided conviction. He was thoroughly suspicious of the balancing acts of college-trained people who could go on and on about their opinions, but who then got lost in their fancy talk and delayed, when not avoided, commitments and action. In his experience, such a person never "puts his ass where his mouth is."

And while he talked a pop fundamentalism, this was not where his true emphasis lay. For him believing was a great deal more than claiming a set of propositions, rather it had to do with staking your life on something. This is why feeling is so important. Feeling carries gravity. That is, if you *really* believe something, you will feel it, and if you *really* feel something, you will do something about it. Feeling that does not have consequences is not real feeling. My point here is not to romanticize working people at the point of religious faith. They can be as faithless and faulted as anyone else. Moreover, I do not mean to say there is no thinking and knowing in working-class faith, but the thinking and knowing take on a very different character than that of the college trained. The point here is the difference in the class construction of religious life.

Oral, Not Literate

Closely related to the above is the fact that most working people in the United States are more oral than literate. That is, they have not usually gone to the university. They do not typically engage the world with theory, with conceptualization of an academic kind, and they do not do discourse, if one means by that the language of a specialization learned in the academy. To be sure, the working class thinks! And they do work with concepts. Their talk around work, for example, develops its own language. But let me quickly say the talk of theology is different from that of cement finishing, the talk of literary criticism is different from that of the maintenance people who keep the buildings going, and the talk of the life sciences is different from that of the service people who work in such a wide range of jobs throughout this society.[1]

Working people are more oral, which means that they are far more likely to engage the world in proverbs and stories and relationship thinking. Working class wisdom is made up of a rich range of sayings that are used in a wide diversity of ways. And, the proverbs are wonderful: "If your ass is on fire, don't throw gas on it." Or, the one from a woman in a honky-tonk: "Most of us gals here tonight only got room for one asshole in our jeans."

Ault's study of the Falwell church in Massachusetts lays out in some detail the oral character of that congregation, with its widely used stories, sayings, proverbs, and maxims. These are used "to express all their teachings."[2] The sayings embody key features of oral culture with their use of metaphor, pun, rhyme, and cadence. Such usage not only makes the teachings memorable, but gives them the kind of hyperbole that speaks to their importance. Ault also notes that an oral tradition is not overly burdened with concerns about contradiction or consistency because their use is determined by the ostensible context in which they occur. There is no reason for determining an aphorism's precise meaning outside the particular context of its use.[3]

Oral culture is rich with stories. Such stories do not typically make a point; they *are* the point. By means of stories the world is engaged and explained. If somebody wants to know about God or the family or life, tell a story. The concrete, lived life displayed in story is perhaps the very best way to reach and to communicate in such communities.

Furthermore, in an oral culture the way one approaches questions and issues is not through theoretical perspectives and alternative policy implications. It is done through relationship thinking. By this I mean that in order to discuss an issue one must "put a face on it."[4] One must talk about someone working people know with whom they have positively some empathy, or negatively, someone who personifies the worst kind of act or direction. I have seen this so many times, for example, in working-class churches where the name of one of the saints in a church is used to support a decision or an action. Sometimes these are national figures: a president, Billy Graham, or Mother Teresa, or (dear God) John Wayne. Sometimes it's someone in one's family. The association of such highly valued people with a given point of view makes for a telling argument.

Oral and Electronic Culture

One qualification needs to be made about the oral culture of working people. The emergence of electronic culture in pervasive forms in the last half of the twentieth century has made no little impact on working people. While the coming of the personal computer is often emphasized in the last two decades of the last century, this is more closely related to the privileged than to working people. What has been pervasive with the younger working class is the impact of popular culture and popular music and entertainment. The place of country music and of certain kinds of rock music like that of Bruce Springsteen and others has enormous influence with younger working-class people. These influences are of such significance that today one must think of the younger working class as both oral and electronic.

In his 1982 book Walter Ong described many of the characteristics of oral cultures, but he also noted that electronic culture was a "secondary orality," and that there were similarities between an oral culture and an electronic one, as well as real differences, of course.[5] This combination of the oral and the electronic is a rich one for consideration in working-class life. In this space two areas will have to suffice. The first is a comparison of the practice of gathering in a more traditional working-class oral culture and the current practice of working-class spectacles in newer, electronic settings. We looked above at the practice of gathering and its centrality in working-class life. Such practices can be quite multisensory but not typically in an electronic sense. In contrast, when one now goes to a Reba McEntire, or Tim McGraw, or a Sara Evans or a Bruce Springsteen concert, these spectacles are massive displays of image, sound, beat, percussive light, movement/dance, and include high audience participation. These are not gatherings, but electronic spectacles. Compare a concert by Hank Williams, Sr. fifty years ago or a Loretta Lynn concert of thirty years ago with contemporary events. Performance has gone through an enormous shift in that time. This shift can be seen as well in tractor pulls, sporting events, NASCAR, and wrestling matches.

Electronic spectacle relates to our second consideration about the relation between oral and electronic culture. The characterization of working-class taste as "rowdy and loud at the Twist and Shout" relates to a long-known factor in working-class worship life and in oral culture, to wit, the place of enthusiasm in style. Religious experience—and that of an overt, emotional, intensive kind—is a dominant factor in indigenous worship life for many working people. This focus on experience has a clear resonance in electronic culture. Leonard Sweet has said, for example, that today the issue is not meaning but experience.[6]

I take the point to be here that the search in electronic culture is not for explanation that makes use of a close reading of the semantic meaning of texts, but rather that younger generations are in search of authentic and significant experience. That is, it is not (propositional and explanatory) meaning in words, but meaning as in being touched and moved that is important for these younger adults. Again, while different, this has more than a little resonance with oral culture.

In sum, younger working people today are a combination of oral and electronic culture. Ministry requires renewed attention to the amalgam of practices emerging out of this combination. The implications for the church are enormous. One example: alternative approaches to worship that learn from—not ape—popular culture will be necessary. Literate, academic-styled clergy-led print-oriented worship services will not address younger working-class people today. Rather alternative worship skilled in multisensory electronic practices is the direction of the future. To put it in more traditional language, the liturgy (the work of the people) will seek faithfulness to the Word and pitch tent with the emergent culture already forming around us.[7]

Faith Commitment of the Heart

Finally, working-class religion can be addressed in terms of what I want to call a faith commitment of the heart. This characteristic reverberates with notions about the importance of believing and feeling and the centrality of a deep experiential relation to God. One can encounter this faith commitment of the heart in a comment such as when a working person will say to a pastor or college-trained person something to the effect: "You may know a lot *about* God, but do you really know *God?*" I have heard comments like this many times. It is important in such encounters to get past the temptation to do a critique of someone who seems to imply that they *do* know God and to display the emptiness of such seeming arrogance. Yet, such a course of action will miss something very important about working-class life. Arrogant the comment may sometimes be, nevertheless, it points to something far more substantive and important than is apparent on a surface hearing.

The comment grows out of a lack of confidence in the capacity of anyone to think about God and to have a powerful relationship to God on the basis of what they know and how well they can think. This is, I dare say, a kind of distrust of thinking and knowing as done by the college trained—read this as the privileged. More than this, such a comment concerns the ways in which religious faith takes on its most durable importance. Faith commitment of the heart gets at the rock solid base of what is finally there in terms of religious faith.

Compare it with a widely known characteristic of more privileged middle-class life. Business and professional people typically live in a structure of privilege. This means that if we do what is expected of us in terms of our jobs and their requirements, we will usually remain privileged. Yet, these structures of privilege can be quite constraining, that is, the structure of privilege can be a box of privilege. If we stay in the box, we will keep the salary, the benefits, the pension, and the status flowing. But, many people experience this box of privilege as the residence of an unemployed self, that is, entire areas of a person's life may not be employed and they live out a narrow sliver of who they are. In theological language they are not giving expression to their gifts from God, but are working at careers they "don't mind because you get used to it." Some, of course, find their work almost intolerable. Changing the structure of privilege seems impossible. So what does one do? What many privileged people typically do is to work on their subjectivity. If one cannot change the box, and, if one cannot stand the work, seek to change your attitude or make your interior life richer. Learn more about yourself. Attend more seminars. Do therapy to get in touch with your inner child. It is an understandable thing to do. It is widely practiced among the privileged.

At the same time it is not typically a working-class thing to do. With many working people the issue is not a box of privilege but a treadmill of routine monotony, and that without the privilege. If you quit one job, you may get a worse one, and at less pay. One country song says it well: "Too much month at the end of the money." Working on your innards may well make things worse by increasing awareness and sharpening your outlook for the future. The question becomes how do you endure and what can you count on? I do not want to suggest that working people are merely passive before the deadening nature of the work that many do. Many working people deal with these things with no little ingenuity and courage—and, yes, courage is the word. My mother worked in quality control in a factory for twenty years for the minimum wage in a job she hated. She once told me, "Son, you just can't think about the job. If I did, I would go crazy. I just get in a conversation with the other ladies and try not to think about the work. It makes the day go much faster. You just have to get through the day."[8]

So, then, how does religious faith work in lives like these? It will be more about trust than about conceptualization and more about assurance than about explanation. It will be a lot more like "knowing God than knowing about God." When something "means a lot," such an expression is about being touched or moved, not primarily about semantically conceptualizing the experience or placing it in the categories of a discipline of academic study.

What can be even more frustrating for those of us versed in the academy is that the language used to talk about such things—and working people do talk about such things—will often not make sense to us. That is, the language used is not used in terms of dictionary precision and certainly not in terms of coherence with a theological position. The language is more embedded in the practices of oral culture—and increasingly electronic culture—and seeks not so much precision about the contours of subjective feeling or experience or theoretical position but to point toward an implicit knowing. This implicit knowing grows from events and practices shared with others. These are not conceptualized in theory but invoked by language common to the happenings associated with this kind of knowing.

Hence the language triggers, or, as I indicate above, invokes the memory of the experience. I remember *one* time in four years when Shucks began to tell me about being saved. He spoke about feeling like he "never had before," about "being close to the Lord," and about "knowing that he was saved." These are phrases that come out of an implicit knowing. There is no attempt here at a discursive description of the experiences. These claims are language that comes from knowing an experience, not attempting to represent it accurately.

Therefore, assurance, trust, knowing God, and being undergirded by powerful events sustain the religious faith of working people. These are the convictions that help get you up in the morning, that keep you working at a job without promise, that make it worth sticking with and sticking up for your family, and that, finally, help you make it through the night. It is not hard to understand in this context why there is so little confidence in theory. It participates in the same fancy talk associated with bosses. It sounds like college boys—and increasingly college girls—who show up in the workplace "who don't know shit about how to do anything, but are full of ideas about how I have to do my job."

This kind of faith commitment of the heart, then, is not concerned primarily about a position that can be defended in the whipsaws of academic critique, but about a living trust that can sustain hard life in a world that does not come out right. Such a faith will be oriented toward survival, coping, need, belonging, and identity. To do ministry with working people is to pitch tent with this kind of lived, very concrete logic.

Blue-collar Resistance and the Politics of Jesus

Summary and Conclusion

The realities of social class are going through rapid and fateful changes. Such changes require renewed attention on the part of the church to do ministry with working-class people. In this book the focus of this work is around working-class whites.

The first step of ministry with working-class whites is a sharp awareness of the practices of social inequality and a commitment to work against such practices in oneself, in the church, and in the community. This involves challenge to the practices of class and the politics of distinction.

Yet such ministry is constructive and not only one of fighting against the inequalities of class. The informing image of ministry here is that of the incarnation. It is a ministry that is faithful to the Word of God made flesh. Yet, further, it takes seriously that the Word "pitched tent" in the life, death, and resurrection of Christ. Jesus joined the indigenous practices of the marginalized people of his own time. Pitching tent is, therefore, intrinsic to the incarnation and to incarnational ministry by the church as the body of Christ.

Working-class ministry requires that clergy and lay leadership avoid the imposition of practices alien to working-class life, and to learn instead their indigenous practices. Such learning entails not only a sensitive understanding of and appreciation for these practices, but a commitment to learn the skills intrinsic to them and the passion to put them to faithful use in the life and work of the church. Such a focus on indigenous practices and appreciation of them, of course, does not mean accommodation with practices that are wrong and destructive. To pitch tent is not to pitch in with the principalities and powers in their fallen and unjust ways.

Working-class people engage pervasively in practices of everyday resistance to the social inequalities of class. Incarnational ministry will discover the spaces of this resistance and join it in opposing the unjust and demeaning rituals of inequality. Indeed, to join such practices and to bless them can turn loose the congealed anger of working people in constructive directions for life together. The church that is an alternative community committed to the reign of God, where such resistance is named and honored, is a community that can draw on deep resources of energy from people long abused. The church that is not a cover for the politics of class, status, and power is one where a populist anarchism can find a worthy aim in the church as a radical alternative to the principalities and powers of the world.

Finally, ministry to working-class whites will deepen its appreciation for their practices of faith and its expression. A faith language of the heart is a vital and authentic response to God's grace. Lives that express their love of God in believing that feels deeply and in feeling that is the mark of conviction are surely not to be faulted for their lack of discursive, explanatory power in a faith that claims justification by faith through grace. Moreover, for people whose lives may never be far from chaos, a faith that stresses surviving, coping, need, belonging, and identity cannot be faulted where trust in God and an assurance of divine care are couched in an implicit knowing. Indeed, this kind of trust may be the most sustaining response to God in a world that does not come out right. At the same time, faithful practices operating with an implicit knowing are not thoughtless or lacking in complexity, but rather can find expression in churches that are compassionate, that are alternative communities of resistance, that seek justice, and that base their confidence and hope in the God who emptied self and took the form of a carpenter. In the spirit of these comments we need to look more specifically at what this church looks like. We turn here in the next chapter.

Chapter 5

THE POLITICS OF JESUS

*T*his book begins with the claim that the church that follows the incarnation of Christ will pitch tent with the indigenous practices of working-class life. The reason for such a claim is my conviction that pitching tent is intrinsic to the Christian faith and to incarnate ministry. There are four senses of this that I want to pick up on here.

First, when Christ pitched tent with the marginal people of first-century Palestine, he joined them in their oppressed circumstances as a people ruled by Rome. He joined a subjugated people. To join people oppressed is to know the practices of oppression. It is neither to blink at the force of such injustice nor to metaphorize it away into some spiritualism that can turn stifling economic violations into a "failure to think positively."

Second, what does such a move look like today in a church that seeks to join white working-class Americans? At the very least it means that the church places its witness at the center of the practices of class. That is, the church undergoes a self-emptying that places its mission with working people in the live-a-day practices of giving and not getting respect, of taking and not giving orders, and of deference to others whose demeanor tells them they are "no people." My point, of course, is not that the church sides with the practices of inequality, but that it refuses protection from these practices. The church that seeks invulnerability will distance itself from the very lives of working people and its life will take on the abstract character of disengaged witness.

Third, some of this can be done easily. For example, it means giving up or not taking up the with-it notions of church life that seem so prominent now. I think particularly of the advocacy of "entrepreneurship" where pastors and lay leadership are supposed to take on the characteristics of highly innovative capitalists. Surely alert working-class people must say to themselves that the ideology that took their jobs has now come to the local congregation. What could be worse than a pastor who sees self as some Donald Trump or Martha Stewart of the working class, who will turn a local congregation into a marketing scheme selling the gospel? Or, one who turns the life of the church into a complex of commodities playing to the already consumerist mentality of this culture (not absent from the working class, I might add)? In a world where working people are told every day that they are fresh meat whose labor is sold on the market battlefield of capitalist greed, shall pastors then embody entrepreneurial managerial lifestyles and promote selling of the gospel, thereby losing its central claim as gift and identifying, at the least, with the metaphors of a capitalism that have brought them to the current state of affairs? We might as well also develop church practices that use metaphors of downsizing and outsourcing as ways of making discipleship leaner and more competitive. This is not pitching tent; it is setting up camp with the enemy.

Fourth, this self-emptying requires a church that, when doing ministry with working people, divests itself of the external practices of America's professional and managerial classes, for example, the horrendous psychobabble of affluent, introspective "autonomous selves," the "strategic planning" that has already done more than enough to control working-class lives, and arrogant misuses of pop psychologies and other behavioral disciplines that bring a professional and managerial bias with them and propose analyses, categories, and prescriptive suggestions out of touch with the lives of working-class people.

The Church as the Teller and Performer of the Story

Still, avoiding consumerist-peddling metaphors and pitching tent is not enough. In the incarnation the Word of God became flesh. The church as the body of Christ not only joins the indigenous practices of a people but is called to make visible and embody the Word made flesh in Jesus. By its practices of worship, sacrament, witness, justice, and peace, the church incarnates the Word.

To say it another way, Jesus not only joins the world, but forever changes the story of the world. To be sure, his story is rooted in ancient Israel. Its prophetic tradition is especially formative in his life and his teaching.[1] At the same time, his death upon the cross as the messiah is a radically new departure and reveals with revolutionary clarity the messianic vocation that claimed him. This is the messiah who turns down the political power of the principalities and powers, crowd-titillating miraculous feats, and bread-and-circus routines so popular with the masses. His response is nonviolent and nonresistant. He "never said a mumblin' word."

In the cross he takes on the principalities and powers. They throw at him everything they have: jail, condemnation by religious leaders, trumped-up charges, a kangaroo court, mockery, torture, and finally the death penalty. The Roman government destroys him. And God answers with resurrection. The powers are defeated and their final destiny is revealed in a world where ultimately God rules, and rules in the way so disclosed in Jesus of Nazareth. Indeed, we see in Jesus "the revelation in the life of a real man of the character of God himself."[2]

The Jesus movement called out a band of disciples and followers. Except for a few women, his followers are terrorized and scattered by his execution. Yet, on the third day, word spreads that the tomb is empty, that he has appeared to the disciples, that he is not dead but alive. The world is now changed. It is no longer a theater of no exits, but a world where a door is always open, even in the terrors of history and in the seeming finality of death itself. Neither of these closes off the ultimate options still in the hands of God. God bats last.

Later, at a strange gathering of an extraordinarily wild range of people, the Holy Spirit descends upon this event and the church is born. A new community is called into being. It is to be the body of Christ in the world. From its birth the church will draw on the power and guidance of the Holy Spirit, and it has the promise of that Spirit throughout all of time. With the leading of this Spirit the church is empowered to be the incarnation of Christ in the world, the body of Christ.

This involves at least two things in this context. First, the job of the church is to tell this amazing story of what God has done. The church, then, is at its very heart a storyteller. As storyteller, the church is witness to the Holy Spirit as the indirect presence of Christ. This is an indirect presence that relates not only to that of being with the church but also to engagement of the Holy Spirit with the events of the world and of human history. The job of the church is always to place the events of history in the story of God, not to place the story of God in the events of history. For example, our work is not to place the nation-state in the role of bearer of the meaning of history, but rather that Christ is that bearer. Our ultimate allegiance is not to the state but to Christ.

Second, the task of the church is not only to tell the story as witness, but to be that story. The church is to be a visible witness to God's story.[3] This underscores the point that the Christian faith is the way of life of a community, not merely a view of life. It is a lived witness that is formed by God's story. It is a journeying in God's story. It is following out an itinerary of living between the times. We live with the confidence that Christ has come and will come again. The story has an end. It is not mere infinite ongoingness. It is not world without purpose or aim. It is a world in which the reign has come in Christ and one in which the fulfillment and completion of nature and history will come in Christ's return.

Therefore I do not want to pose the question of how the church can be relevant to working-class life. Rather, the question is one of how the stories and liturgies of oppression can be placed in a more encompassing story of what God has done in Christ. It is a question of how the church as the body of Christ outnarrates the stories of class and offers an alternative to the practices of inequality.

But let me be clear, I am especially concerned that the church not do what has too often been done in the mission work, that is, to bring an external culture—in the case of working people, the culture of middle-class business and professional America—and attempt to impose it, whether such imposition be conscious or not. In this case I want the church to pitch tent with the indigenous practices of working people. I want the church to join them in their resistance to the practices of inequality. At the same time, by placing these practices in the story of what God has done in Christ, the story of class is placed in a new and radically different story, and it comes with practices of its own. To begin these moves I start with the church as tactic.

Working-class Resistance and the Church as Tactic

In de Certeau's discussion of the *places* of the powerful and the *spaces* the powerless set up in those spaces, he makes a telling distinction between strategies and tactics. Strategy is a practice of the powerful. With their capacities for setting boundaries they can establish places that they control, things like "a business, an army, a city, a scientific institution." These places serve as "a base" from which the powerful can engage external others "(customers or competitors, enemies, the county surrounding the city, objectives and objects of research, etc.)." In strategies the powerful attempt to set apart their " 'own' place, the place of [their] own power and will, from an 'environment.' " In de Certeau's view these places are "a triumph of place over time," and "a mastery of places through sight." Strategies involve a certain kind of knowledge; actually such knowledges help establish places to give them boundaries of appropriate jurisdiction. Thus, this kind of power produces a knowledge even as such knowledge is a precondition of this kind of power. Through these means, the powerful can make plans and develop long-term goals.[4]

In contrast, tactics are a practice of the weak and the powerless. As we saw above, the farmer who lost his farm and had to go to the mill town continued to farm but now in a space within the place of the mill. When the powerful build places, the powerless set up spaces in the midst of them. Certeau sees such tactics as operating " 'within the enemy's field of vision.' " The powerless do not have the means to establish a place of their own. The powerless do not have "the options of planning general strategy and viewing the adversary as a whole within a distinct, visible, and objectifiable space." They operate in "isolated actions," dealing with things as they come. They grab whatever opportunities come along. They "make use of the cracks" in the world of power, where surveillance breaks down or where a ruse or a trick can take temporary advantage of the panopticon [surveillance] propensities of established order. A tactic as used by the powerless is "a guileful ruse." [5] Hence, "a tactic is determined by the absence of power just as a strategy is organized by the postulation of power." [6]

For example, Dudley reports on the games played on the shop floor by auto workers and the way these take the form of tactical resistance. One good instance of the use of tactics occurs when an operator of a complex machine fixes it so it won't run. So they send for an electrician. The electrician knows that the operator understands the machine much better than he does. Without the operator's help, he cannot fix it. If the operator is asked what the problem is and he simply says it won't work, this leaves the electrician in the spot of not knowing where to start. He is at a loss with a machine that may be a half-block long and have hundreds of wires. One electrician simply asks the operator how long he wants the machine down, and promises that he will keep it down that long. The electrician says to the operator. "If you want the machine down, how long do you want it down? I'll keep it down as long as you want; just don't make me work any harder than I have to. If you want it down for an hour, I'll keep it down for an hour."[7] The operator will then tell him where the problem is, and he can go to work, staying within the agreement between the two of them.

There are also plenty of examples of tactics in local congregations. I think of the way many working people make the back row of the sanctuary a space in the place of the church. Or, the way that some will work with the Scouts and occupy—and sometimes it is an occupa- tion—the Scout room, but will hardly darken the door- way of the church for worship. I also recall craftspeople who take over responsibility for the plumbing or the electricity or the furnace of the church and turn it into their space. Or, of course, church groups—usually women—may take the kitchen as a place within the space of the church building. To be sure, working peo- ple are not the only people who do such things, but they are major players in these tactical expressions in local churches.

But I want to go farther than this and to look at the church itself as a tactic to see what this would look like. With the demise of Christendom a good case can be made for the role of the church to be more thoroughly one of tactic. We live in a time in which the church no longer has the legitimacy in the wider society it once did. One can bewail this or look upon it as a desirable setting in which to pursue a more faithful course of action by the church as an alternative to the dominant culture. This is not new in church history. The role of the Anabaptists and the left wing of the Reformation certainly are examples of such a witness. Furthermore, a good argument can be made that the church has more constructive influence when it has not had the endorsement of the dominant culture but developed alternative structures and approaches as a minority, even a disenfranchised one, within dominant arrangements. I believe we are in that kind of context today, but my position is not basically a strategic one. That is, not only do I not bewail the loss of the Constantinian church, I believe the more faithful and therefore more intrinsic position of the church ought to be that of an alternative to the dominant principalities and powers. This will be strange territory for mainline churches today, but a necessary one and a more faithful one. At the same time, my aim here is to look at working-class churches as this kind of alternative. A tactical approach to the working-class church makes an important connection between Christian faith and working-class lives.[8]

In reading Dudley's work she reports on "a culture of the mind" that characterized the new business and professional class that conflicted with and named as outdated and nostalgic "the culture of the hand" that characterized the autoworkers of Kenosha. The former played an active role in the demise of the auto plant and gave legitimation to Chrysler to close the plant. Probably the loss of the plant was just one more case of global capitalism forever changing a local community in the direction of its bottom-line social Darwinist goals. Yet, I wonder what it would have meant had there been a church of working people who sharply contested the strategies of the new class professionals, who challenged their ideology, who set up spaces of resistances in the face of such professional moves and redefinitions of the city. What if there had been a church that set up a sacred space alternative to, and in active resistance to, the actions of the powers. In this instance I doubt that it would have changed the closing of the plant but I do believe it would have been a major resource in helping the autoworkers cope more adequately with the sense of loss and self-degradation that occurred.

Living Out of Control and Relativizing Loss

So let us examine a few aspects of what it means to be the church as tactic. The first thing to be said is that the church is a community of resistance taking up spaces in the midst of the places of the world. The church is not in a position of control, but rather has the mission of living out of control. God does not control the world by means of coercion but by means of the cross. To know that God is God and not us and to know the God we know in the cross is to renounce coercion. It is to give up on illusions of omnipotence that we can make the world and history turn out right. This does not mean that we ignore deliberate efforts to seek justice, but rather we do not sell out to utilitarian efforts to construct justice that betray the God of the cross known in Christ Jesus.[9] To live out of control is to trust God's story to be faithful to the mission of keeping that story going. In that process it uses liturgical space to subvert the conventional understandings and relationships of the world.

With working-class people the church as tactic refuses the practices of inequality and rejects the pretensions of status in its own life. In liturgical space I think of liturgies that explicitly proclaim the biblical word such as that in Philippians 3 where Paul lays out his qualifications as one circumcised, as a member of the people of Israel, of the tribe of Benjamin, a Hebrew born of Hebrews, a Pharisee, and a persecutor of the church, and one blameless under the law. But he then says: "Whatever gains I had, these I have come to regard as loss because of Christ. More than that, I regard everything as loss because of the surpassing value of knowing Christ Jesus my Lord. For his sake I have suffered the loss of all things, and I regard them as crap [*skybala* in the Greek, "dung"], in order that I may gain Christ" (NRSV, paraphrased).[10]

I think here of autoworkers in Kenosha. There is no compelling evidence that the craftsmanship of the Kenosha workforce declined before the loss of the plant. If anything their work improved in attempts to save it. The workers had placed their faith in the idea that good work will be rewarded. They believed that this tradition, however, had been overruled. Such an abrogation indicated that the world was now without rhyme or reason.[11] A picture like this is not unique to the role of power in changing the makeup of places of power in the seeking of self-interest. It is, if anything, common. Yet, while it will not take away the suffering, it can be a powerful thing for the church and its people to say that "I have suffered the loss of all things, and I regard them as crap."

I do not mean to suggest some mindless palliative here, but rather to address the fact that in a loss of this magnitude a faith community can relativize such loss and place it in a larger story. Also, I do not mean to suggest that nothing else is done. If the move is only a declaration to assuage subjective feeling, it is not faithful. A church as tactic is also a survivor community looking for ways people can make the moves and find the resources to rebuild a life. That is, some of the things happening to working people today cannot be bent to avoid dislocation and disruption. In sad circumstances like these a larger story is needed, one that can address and relativize damage and loss so as not to give in to futility and destitution. This is not pie in the sky, but finding bread enough to continue the journey, to go on.

The second thing to be noted about the church as tactic is its ad hoc character. In ways analogous to the unsystematic character of working-class resistance, the church will take things as they come. There is a wonderful quality about living out of control so that one is not compulsively compelled by the need to straighten out the things of the world. It is an enormous freedom in being the people of God and engaging in the practices intrinsic to the faith while knowing that things will never be finally finished while we live between the

times. For reasons like these, I love Stanley Hauerwas'
notion of "doing theology one brick at a time."

> In a sense, I am a theologian who still works like a brick-
> layer. You can only lay one brick at a time. Moreover,
> each brick you lay is different. Though bricks look quite
> uniform, and they often are, there are always variations
> that force the bricklayer to cut head joints in a manner
> necessary for the bond to be true. In other words, you
> have to adjust how you lay the next brick because of what
> happened when you laid the previous brick and, at the
> same time, in anticipation of the one to come. Moreover,
> bricklayers may work from a blueprint, but the way the
> brick must be laid often means the relation between what
> is originally drawn and what results defies easy compari-
> son. . . . Composing essays is something like doing theol-
> ogy one brick at a time.[12]

So it is also for the church as tactic with the working
class. It is called to live out of control. It is to live in the
spaces in the midst of places of power, means living in
the church and dealing with the world "one brick at a
time." I do not mean a complacency here or an easy
accommodation. I will discuss other moves by the
church as tactic later, but it is key that the church be a
tactic and take on issues as they arise.

Basic to the gravity of the ad hoc character of the
church as tactic is the unpredictability of things. Life is
profoundly unpredictable. We do not know what is
coming next. The emphasis in the church as tactic is to
engage in the practices intrinsic to the faith, to form
ourselves as God's people, the body of Christ, and to

base our lives eschatalogically as a people who live between the times.

The third thing to be said about the church as tactic is its capacity for improvisation. Samuel Wells offers the theatrical practice of improvisation as an approach to Christian ethics. He sees it as a pattern for Christian imagination. In theatrical improvisation there is a move of "overacceptance" in which one actor takes the comments or actions of a previous actor or actors but then places them in a context that is much more encompassing and compelling, one that the first actor could not have imagined. Wells sees this practice as a way to face fate and turn it into destiny. That is, improvisation takes what is given and turns it into a gift. It is a more fully orbed way of taking lemons and turning them into lemonade. In this approach to Christian ethics we are not so much called to decide what is right as to be formed in the habits, really the art, of faithfully accepting fate as a gift. So that the church, immersed in God's story, takes the givens of the world and turns them into opportunities to be faithful.

Wells understands that this may seem too passive and accommodative, but his point rather is that overacceptance is a "witness-full" way to challenge the seeming necessities of the world. It is a way to immerse the church in the eschatological shape of history. I love one illustration Wells uses when he reminds us of the story of the steel workers in the movie *The Full Monty*, who were "stripped of their dignity by the experience of unemployment. They overaccepted their condition by developing a thriving male-stripper routine."[13] He, of course, does not suggest that this is a move of Christian ethics but an example of overacceptance.

In instances like this he sees overacceptance as a primary tactic by which the church can outnarrate the world, a subject we shall turn to later.

In sum, I have named three moves illustrative of the church as tactic. These moves are not exhaustive of a church taking up spaces in the places of the powerful, but they are key and suggest directions for the working-class church. In this focus on the church as tactic we need also to look at two basic characteristics of the church that will embody such moves. We look at these next.

"Gonna Live with Jesus in the End"

Wynonna Judd sings a song written entitled "Live with Jesus."[14] The song opens with the line that she's "seen a lot of trouble at my door." This is no abstract notion of subjective struggle taken alone. She is not merely ogling her gut. She deals with trouble that hangs around, that stays as close as your door. She tells us that not a day has passed without her being poor. She's been through hard times and she's lost the person most dear to her. Her bones are "tired and old," but she will meet her Savior and he will "deem" her soul, and she will "live with Jesus in the end."

It is a very New Testament thing to say. When I hear that song I think of Paul in Romans 8:18: "I consider that the sufferings of this present time are not worth

comparing with the glory about to be revealed to us."
And then later, "For in hope we were saved" (8:24a). I
realize the song can be heard as pie in the sky by and
by, but I do not hear it that way, and certainly Paul does
not call for that move. Rather, I contend that it is a different way of envisioning the world and history.

This song reflects living in a world between the
times. Christ has come and Christ will come again. We
live in the interval between those two events. Again, as
I shall attempt to indicate, this is not a vision that calls
us to do nothing, but it does call the church to a very
different story, and a very different politics, the politics
of Jesus.[15] This politics addresses a radically different
approach to the practices of inequality and to the practices of resistance of working people. While it pitches
tent with these, it places them in a different story with
its own practices. It can respond to populist anarchism,
but it is an anarchism of its own. It is sensitive to the
religious expression of working-class spirituality, but it
places such things in a larger story. It begins with the
centrality of Jesus Christ and his calling of a new community grafted onto the story of ancient Israel.

The Church as Family of God

A second characteristic of the church as tactic in the
working class is the church as family. In the research of
James Ault we see how much the lives of the working
people of the Falwell Baptist Church are based in the
extended family relationships of that community and
the impact these relationships have on the everyday
affairs of that congregation. We also see how different

this is from the lives of business and professional people who are more individualistic in orientation with their tendencies to leave home to pursue career.

This form of life makes working people much more open to church life that takes on familylike characteristics. Craig Carter in his fine book on John Howard Yoder's social ethics states that Yoder's model of the church is "modeled on an extended family in a local community." Carter sees this as possessing the possibility of being a "viable (nonoppressive because freely chosen) alternative to liberal individualism."[16]

Yoder makes a good deal of the importance of the voluntary character of church life. It allows for a disciplined church life because the discipline is self-imposed. This means, too, that individuals don't so much make up their own individualistic minds (no one really does that), but rather work as an extended family might, only one now working to be faithful to Christ and seeking the guidance of the Holy Spirit.

I want to take this a step further. In terms of the realities of class, the church as family can be a sharp alternative to the practices of inequality. When people are brothers and sisters in Christ, the possibility is at least there that the liturgies of status can be subverted so that respect is given in the Lord. Orders are not given to individuals but rather the body itself makes decisions and entreats people to carry out actions, and so that coercion is ruled out of life in the church.[17]

As an alternative to practices of class, the church is a visible witness to the community in which it exists. By its very existence it is engaged in mission, suggesting by this that such a community, such a politics is radically at variance from what is usually found in our culture. But more than that, it offers new ways for people to be together, new and alternative ways for people to work together and get things done. Obviously, this needs more substance than mere declaration and I will develop these notions more in terms of practices that embody these alternatives than simply claiming they ought to be.

For now, let me say that nothing will speak more to working people than a congregation that is an alternative to the principalities and powers of class. It is not necessary that class be ended in the world, it's not likely to happen soon, but it is possible that an alternative community can be a foretaste of another, radically different form of life. Basic to this church is the craft tradition of discipleship.

Chapter 6

THE CRAFT TRADITION OF DISCIPLESHIP

O ne day in the oil field we were laying a pipeline. The gang pusher, the leader of the gang, told me to give a try to "stabbing the pipe." This was something I had not done before, though I had seen others do it in the few days I had been in the field. When you lay pipe by hand, you prop the end of the pipe already laid up on the edge of a board about a foot high. Someone then takes the next pipe and inserts it into the collar of the pipe already laid. My job from that pipe's other end is then to "stab" the pipe, which means I have to aim my joint of pipe so that it will screw straight into the collar of the pipe propped up on the board. These pipes are two inches in diameter, twenty feet long and weigh two hundred pounds, so I have to get the threads lined up just right while wrestling with this pipe that outweighs me by twenty pounds. It does not help that the pipe bends a little, making it even more difficult to line them up exactly. Moreover, I am using a small wrench, which has a chain that wraps around the pipe. It also has a handle that I must turn once the pipe is lined up, while holding the pipe at the right angle with my other hand. You screw with one hand and hold the pipe in place with the other.

The first few times you do this, it is not easy. I am obviously inept and struggling. I am also known as the "college boy." This is my summer job earning money to make my way through school, and the gang delights in assigning me tasks that either I cannot do or cannot do well, or that cannot be done by anyone. (In the latter case, every new recruit to the oil field is sent off to get the "sky hooks," which, of course, do not exist.)

As I wrestle that pipe, Shucks Burt, a trucker in the gang who revels in my incompetence, is laughing and states the issue with no little accuracy.

"Hey, college boy, there's a right way to do that and all the other ways are wrong and yore opinion don't mean a damned thing."

The entire gang collapses in laughter.

This remains my most vivid experience with the craft tradition of knowing. The longer I live the more important it has become not only in connecting pipe and things of a laboring kind but in academic thought as well: philosophical, theological, or social. It is a wonderful critique of notions that we must first get our ideas together and then go and apply them. The craft tradition takes a radically different approach. In what follows I want to make connections between the craft tradition as it is found in so much of working-class life and Christian mission and ministry. We can use the wisdom of Shucks Burt to help us here.

Perhaps the first thing to be said is that if you are going to lay pipe, you do not start with your opinion or some universal notion of reason or some general kind of knowledge. While no one begins to lay pipe from scratch, nevertheless, to lay pipe you have to pay attention to pipe. You have to know weight and balance and aim. You have to have the feel and the practiced use of wrenches, and so on. You see, in the craft tradition of knowing, our minds are not adequate to the task until we have conformed ourselves to the objects on which we are working.[1]

So it is also that, in the life of the church, one does not begin with generalized notions of religious knowledge. Karl Barth rigorously argued that God made Self a Subject in Jesus Christ as a revelation of the character of God. Any true knowledge we have comes as the gift of God in Jesus Christ. Indeed, it is the free act of God making Self known as Subject in Christ. We do not know how to know God conceptually on our own terms. Any knowledge we have of God in human terms is knowledge from the world in Barth's understanding. Hence, I argue that in the working-class church we begin with Jesus Christ and his centrality for the church and for our life together. To be the church, the central focus of our attention is Jesus Christ. To know Christ is to be formed by him. In the language of craft Christ is both the object to which we are to form ourselves and our mentor; to know Christ is to apprentice with and for him.

It is my observation that working people have much less trouble with accepting the revelation of God in

Christ than the people who went off to the university. I blame this failure on the fact that the modern university for so long so thoroughly accepted the Enlightenment as the dominant historical and cultural formation of its existence: its privileging of modern science, universal reason, the free autonomous individual, the nation-state, and the search for foundations of knowing in reason and experience, among other things.[2]

One result of this is that the dominant themes of the Enlightenment make any particular faith tradition an illusion (Freud) or an opiate (Marx and Feuerbach) or a local expression of a more universal religion (Joseph Campbell). Other times, however, it results in some other generalization that not only denies or relativizes the claim or places it in some more "universal" form of human experience, but also obscures that tradition by forcing it into another set of categories or moving it into more abstract and general propositions.[3]

Thus, most people who go off to the university tend to be socialized into that world. They become pop cosmopolitans. These are the business and professional people who seek churches that let them think what they want to think and encourage them to keep open minds, aka "free autonomous individuals" who are so thoroughly absorbed in the modern story of the Enlightenment that it is impossible for them to maintain an open mind because they are so committed to the categories and thought of the modern period. The result typically is that most live an unexamined faith of the first order. This "faith" and its "values" are located in historical and cultural forms of life that are so encompassing that they contradict the very notion of free autonomous individuals possessed with universal reason. Such is the devotion of a great many to Enlightenment commitments.

Let me be clear here. It is not my aim to take away the opportunities of people to pursue ideas and to think. My concern rather is the ways we cannot think because we are so conditioned by the assumptions of the Enlightenment and see these as some kind of objectivity. I contend that people always already think within a story, e.g., the Enlightenment story or the Christian story or some other. What we need to do is to identify the stories that form the cultural and historical conditions of our thought, to criticize those, and to participate actively in a tradition that is, as Alasdair MacIntyre states, a socially embodied, historically extended argument.[4] I certainly have no desire that the church become theocratic through the powers of the state. In fact, I think that the church needs to give up on coercion.[5] At the same time, my effort here is to engage working-class resistance from within the story of God as that is known in the church.

The people who often boss working people at one level or another are typically formed by the Enlightenment story, albeit in a pop or implicit way, but it is deeply engrained in the culture and the ways they see the world. Working people have heard way too much universalizing from such leaders. (They don't call it "universalizing" but rather "fancy talk" or just "bullshit.") They also know that such talk tends to serve interests that are not those of working people. Perhaps this is one reason they are more open to hear a biblical faith not filtered through the Enlightenment.[6]

The second thing to be said about a craft tradition is that the stress is not on knowing as knowing but rather on knowing how to do things.[7] Again, this is an approach to knowing that makes enormous connections with working-class jobs. Dudley in her study of autoworkers found that a person's value had little to do with their position or educational achievements, but rather that "individual ability is demonstrated by what people do—by their actions rather than words, by deeds rather than fancy degrees, and most important, by the tangible results of their labor."[8] Furthermore, the fact that one must be formed by pipe in order to lay it has fascinating connections to Barth's understanding that if we are to know Christ, we must be formed by him. It is a connection open to a wide range of narrative witness with working people.

When this kind of knowing is contrasted with the bosses' knowing, it engages working people at the point of the sharpest kinds of resistance. I remember one day in the oil field we were to lay a pipeline into a header (a header is typically a larger pipe into which a number of other pipes are fed or joined). The problem was that there was a snarl of pipes already laid in front of the header, making the approach unusually difficult. When the engineer, fresh out of college, came out, he had already sketched a drawing of how he wanted the pipe to enter the header. His sketch, however, was abstract and did not take into account the snarl of pipe that blocked that kind of an approach. When the gang pusher (the leader) asked him about the design, the engineer simply said, "Let's just stay with the drawing" but did not actually attend to the problem the pusher wanted to address. We then laid the pipe as close to the plan as possible but left the final fifteen yards unfinished. The pusher called the engineer out to explain to us how he wanted it to go the rest of the way. When he finally saw the problem, he suggested an alteration to the drawing that the gang had already figured out from the very beginning. The gang was quiet while he was there and quite deferential, but as soon as he left, the air was filled with mockery and derision at his ineptitude.[9]

The third thing to say about the craft tradition of knowing is the importance of skills. Most working-class jobs require skills, and skills require practice. While learning to stab pipe can be done after a few tries, it is but one in an enormous range of skills required to work well in the oil field: being able to operate around and inside oil tanks, maintaining giant compressors that pump gas back into the ground, cleaning complicated machinery or repairing it, replacing ball bearings in a large number of moving parts, knowing how to work and be safe, the arduous range of skills for working on an oil well drilling rig and so on.

So it is in the faith. Stanley Hauerwas has emphasized the importance of learning skills as a member of the body of Christ.[10] There are many such skills, of course, but I will illustrate this with just one example, the skill of reading the Bible. My father finished the fifth grade when he had to quit school to help support his family because his father was murdered. He continued a commitment to self-education that enabled him to "read, write, and do his numbers." But higher education was a threatening thing to him. He was too concerned about his own lack of learning when around people who had been to the university. When he was in his nineties, he took a course on drafting at a community college. According to the professor Dad was making a grade of B well into the semester, but he was so intimidated by being in a college course that the pressure was too much, and he dropped the class.

Yet thirty years before that he drafted and built a creosote plant almost single-handedly. My uncle bought the machinery to set up the plant, and my father who had never worked in that kind of production, nevertheless went off visiting such plants in Mississippi, taking with him a pile of brown paper bags. He went from plant to plant drawing plans on those brown paper bags and went back to Learned, Mississippi, and built a creosote plant that worked! To be sure, it took false starts and practice, most of them on the job, but he built and then learned how to creosote lumber. It was "just a bunch of things" that he "had to learn" and he never "had any question that he could do it."

All his life he loved the Bible. Even when I was in grammar school, he would ask me to come in at night and read the text to him. He especially loved the Psalms and the Gospels. He would have loved to study the Bible more formally, but it was too threatening to him to do it except in Sunday school, where he did not have to perform. I wonder what would have happened if someone—me, for example—had told him that it was just a bunch of skills like building and running a creosote plant and that he could do it on brown paper bags.

A final thing, which is all we have space for here, is the connection between the craft tradition of knowing and the role of apprenticeship learning. Any semi-skilled or skilled trade requires apprenticeship. Even as a roustabout (laborer) in the oil field, I had to learn a great deal by working with and listening to the experienced hands in the gang. It may seem that my father belies apprenticeship learning in his building of and supervising the creosote plant, but he had worked in a wide variety of jobs around machinery, tanks, pumps, gauges, feedback mechanisms, and running line (pipe), so he had done a great deal of apprenticeship learning directly relevant to a creosote operation, although he often spoke of the immense amount of trial and error he had to do in building the plant.

Likewise, life in the church is the learning of a great many skills: worship, prayer, Bible reading, confession, thanksgiving, servanthood, caring for others, living peaceably, witnessing, Eucharistic practice, being just, and many others. To approach these practices as skills to be learned through apprenticeship would be a very helpful way to address working people. I noticed as a pastor of a working-class congregation that the Scouting program drew a good many people who would not go to worship or Sunday school. After no little observation of this pattern, I came to believe that one of the reasons was the merit-badge approach to learning in Scouts. This program was oriented toward learning different skills and doing so through apprenticeship to the Scout leaders. It had a direct draw to working-class youth, as well as to their mentors.

I have often wondered what it would be like to develop an entire Christian education program around the development of skills in the church and the larger community and to do so with mentors working with the students. Also, this would need to be done precisely in the language of skills and apprenticeship so that the connections between working-class life and the work of the church are direct, indigenous, and faithful.

Craft Work with the Bible

A key issue for working people, especially in Protestant churches, is the use of the Bible. While a good many are fundamentalist, most clearly are not. I have discussed elsewhere that nonfundamentalist working-class people can come off like fundamentalists in their dislike of criticism of the Scripture. This has more to do with their loyalty to the Bible than to a more formal or systematic way of interpreting it.[11] A good many have not read it, at least not very much, but may still be quite committed to it in the sense of wanting to protect it. They also don't have much "truck" with elitist, abstract, theoretical treatments that seem to be bent on getting out from under its teaching.

I am often struck by the loyalty of working people in the church to the Bible and the claim of a theologian like Yoder when he says, "the presence of the text within the community is an inseparable part of the community's being itself. It would be a denial of the community's being itself if it were to grant a need for appeal beyond itself to some archimedean point to justify it."[12] I don't want to equate working-class loyalty to the Bible with Yoder's point of Scripture's basic relationship to the identity of the church because I don't often hear working people talk like that, but there is that unbreakable, substantive tie between the Bible and the church that is exactly right, and here Yoder's point could be heard with gratitude by working people.

Still, working people deserve better than they get in teaching about Scripture, and, fundamentalism, when it has been adopted, has not served the working class well. What is needed instead is something very close to what Yoder has called "biblical realism." By this Yoder means that one presupposes that the Scriptures have a testimony that is coherent and that it is the task of the church to discern. He also uses this term to question those who believe that we can "get behind" the text.[13] Yoder desires therefore to approach the text to see what it has to say to us.

The interpretive job is not to begin by doubting the Scripture, but by doubting the adequacies of our previous understandings of it.[14] The central character of biblical realism with Yoder is a rigorous use of critical tools without, however, knowing in advance "where we want it to fit into a pre-existent larger systematic scheme."[15]

In biblical realism the Scripture does have a unity, but it is one of a story that has a beginning, a middle, and an end. That is, the story goes somewhere, and this aim or end—this somewhere—is read back into the text. That is, the unity is not one in which every part of the text is to be read in the same way with the same gravity or with equal interpretive, formative power. For Yoder there is directionality in the biblical story as it moves from the Old Testament to the New. It moves from promise to fulfillment. Indeed, there is a canon within the canon, but it is not single doctrine, but rather Jesus Christ who stands at the center of Scripture.[16]

Michael Cartwright states that Yoder understands that there is mediation of the biblical text in any use of Scripture, that is, we do not read the text without interpretation, but "Yoder believes that where the free church is concerned the mediation involved in the recovery of the apostolic idiom remains *integrally related* to the way Scripture has been appropriated in the past by the faithful church." Cartwright then quotes Yoder wherein Yoder argues that a contemporary believing community "participates imaginatively, narratively, in the past history as her own history, thanks to her historians, but also thanks to her poets and prophets."[17] Yoder maintains that today's believing church will come up with something "quite original yet essentially like what the faith had meant before." As James Wm. McClendon Jr. states in his *Ethics: Systematic Theology*, "the story *now* echoes the story *then*, *is the story then*."[18]

This connection between the church and the reading of Scripture is crucial in Yoder. He maintains that we cannot address the Scripture "apart from people reading it" nor "apart from the specific questions" readers bring to it. To do so violates the very reason "we have been given the Holy Scriptures." Yoder argues that an "isolated" biblical passage cannot carry meaning by itself alone, but rather "only when it is read by someone and then only when that reader and the society in which she or he lives can understand the issue to which it speaks." He then states:

> Thus the most complete framework in which to affirm the authority of Scripture is the context of its being read and applied by a believing people that uses its guidance to respond to concrete issues in their witness and obedience.[19]

I have problems with Yoder's label of biblical realism for his position. My difficulties center around the mediated character of the Bible, as Yoder admits. My basic concern is that in our mediation of the Scripture, we never get it right. While I certainly believe we can read the Bible faithfully, it is too much to argue that we read with biblical realism. Yet, take away the label, and I find the church powerfully addressed by Yoder's approach to the biblical text.

For this reason I want to provide the label of *biblical craft* to the substantive arguments of Yoder's view. Such a characterization is not only more attentive to the mediated character of biblical interpretation but also addresses issues of tradition and the corporate nature of the church. So I now want to name several ways in which Yoder's approach addresses the working class, especially working-class resistance.

First, the Bible as story, really as inspired story, is key. In chapter 3 I noted the oral character of working-class people. They are people of the story. Storytelling is a basic practice; it is the way that truth is crystallized and communicated. Moreover, the work of a craft is one of a story, the story of its origins and development, the history of its accomplishments and legacies. To speak of Scripture as a story to be learned and as a story to be lived out, to be reenacted, to be performed, to be engaged in the craft of living life faithful to Christ resonates across the existence of working-class life. I think here particularly of the believing and feeling character of working-class faith. This is a measure of the conviction, the authenticity of working-class religious commitment. To place believing and feeling in the frame-work of performing Scripture—putting Scripture to work—adds to and enriches these measures of genuine conviction.[20]

Second, to work with Scripture as a craft to be learned, places Bible study and biblical living in a powerfully legitimative frame. It makes it clear, at least when used in terms of the work of the church, that Bible study is not merely an academic enterprise in which one garners intellectual views in a status preserve, but rather, like a craft, is a whole way of being in the world. It is not merely a view of life but a way of life. It is not the attempt to imitate the fancy ideas of the college trained but to see Christ as the center of the

Bible and to render the church's witness Christlike in the everyday life of making it through the day and through the night.

Third, the craft tradition of Bible study and biblical action underscores the role of the church as the "trade body." It speaks to the required corporate character of any craft and the solidarity necessary not only to its execution but also to its range and reach of knowing and to its ongoing continuation.

Fourth, biblical study as craft offers a way out of fundamentalism and a severe evangelicalism that attempts to freeze the text. Such views are not unlike working with an instruction manual doing everything exactly as it says. Such things cripple a craft, taking away its art and improvisation and rendering it wooden and regimented with too many instructions to follow and no apprenticed learning to know what is most important. Such approaches do not know the difference between obeying a skewed selection of texts from a topical concordance and working in the energies and flows of a full-blown craft. They, therefore, go by the book and, in the case of the Bible, lose the book.

In this connection let me then suggest some moves in biblical craft as ways the working-class church can interpret the Scripture. I will use metaphoric language as substitutes for more academic language. Such usage makes biblical study more accessible for working people without sacrificing an interpretive integrity.

The first of these is the move to tell a better story, i.e., to "outnarrate" the world. This move takes as basic that the narrative of Scripture is more real than the claims of the secular world. I do not mean here that we accept a three-story view of the universe or that we support creationism in the schools, or that we read the Bible "literally" (the reading of any text is mediated). But I do mean that the Scripture is inspired, not verbally, but narratively as it is read by the church under the guidance of the Holy Spirit. I follow Yoder here in his conviction that "the reality portrayed in the biblical narrative is more real than the reality depicted in other narratives."[21]

I think here of the Apostle Paul's view of the reconciliation wrought in Christ. In Paul's thought Christ has reconciled Jews and Gentiles, and these two groups include everyone! This is the monumental work that God has done in Christ. He says, "From now on . . . we regard no one from a human point of view" (2 Cor 5:16). For anyone who "is in Christ, there is a new creation . . . everything has become new! All this is from God, who reconciled us to himself through Christ, and has given us the ministry of reconciliation; that is, in Christ God was reconciling the world to himself" (2 Cor 5:17-19). This story of God's act in Christ makes the church ambassadors for Christ who are entrusted with the message of reconciliation. This is the story the church is called to put to work in its life and in the world. This is a radical alternative to the story of class. It is a basic challenge to a world that continually defines working people as mindless, redneck, white trash.

In the background of my thought here is the work of Eugene D. Genovese on slavery and the world the

American slaves built. In this space the slaves were not "Sambas" but the children of God who engaged in a world making as an alternative to slavery.[22] Lawrence W. Levine takes this a step further in his discussion of the way in which the slaves built a "sacred universe." Basic to this resistance were embodied practices that challenged the oppressive world of slavery by means of slave songs, an alternative slave religion with its own forms of black preaching, folk beliefs, magic, and voodoo.[23] White working people do not face slavery, of course, but they do undergo the "worlds of pain" of lower-class life.[24] Basic to the ministry of the church is the construction of a community of faith that lives a different story that turns people who were no people into God's people (1 Pet 2:10).

This very story also calls into question working-class failure and sin as well. We can no longer regard racial ethnic people and women from a human point of view. The reconciliation God has brought in Jesus Christ has broken down these divisions, and the church is called to live the story of reconciliation. In this story is the intrinsic claim that in Christ "There is no longer Jew or Greek, there is no longer slave or free, there is no longer male and female; for all of you are one in Christ Jesus" (Gal 3:28).

The second point is what I will call a "sort of like" approach to biblical interpretation.[25] I mean in this to use "sort of like" in a technical sense. That is, the world of the New Testament and our own are quite different. For example, we cannot simply move from the three-story universe of biblical times to our own. Yet, there are great analogies or resemblances or parallels or cor-relative aspects between the New Testament and our time. Working with the biblical text then requires the church to use our imaginations to find the analogues, the "sort of like" character, between the New Testament portrayal of Jesus and the ways we are addressed by it today. The crucial point here, however, is that this use of analogy by the church is one that attempts to reshape today's world in terms of the lord-ship of Christ, and not to make Jesus a figure from the past who is either incidental or elective to these matters or, perhaps, downright irrelevant. I appreciate in this regard Yoder's point that there is a canon within the canon of the New Testament, but it is not a doctrine or some other theme, but Jesus Christ. So the Scripture is read directionally, i.e., from the revelation of Christ as the fulfillment of the promises of God in ancient Israel and in the New Testament itself.[26]

For example, Albert Schweitzer in his classic text *The Quest of the Historical Jesus* concludes that the historical Jesus cannot be adequately understood apart from a late Jewish eschatological-apocalyptic view of history. That is, Jesus expected and taught that the kingdom is soon to come and called people to a discipleship shaped decisively by this expectation. Schweitzer draws from this the view that Jesus' teaching represents "an inter-im ethic," i.e., an ethic that applies only to that brief time before the kingdom of God would come in its fullness.[27]

Yoder, however, argues that it is not necessary to give up the eschatological Jesus in doing Christian ethics.

Noting that a number of New Testament scholars challenge the view that late Jewish apocalyptic thought had an imminent end of the world in sight, Yoder argues, following Oscar Cullmann, that in Christ on the cross the basic victory over the principalities and powers—over sin and death and evil—has been won, but that the struggle is not over. It will continue into the indefinite future, but it is a story in which God's reign will prevail. In this sense, we live between the times in a history in which the reign of God has come in Christ, but in which it has not come in its completion. We live in a time of the already but not yet. Nevertheless, it is a story with an end, and we live somewhere in the middle of that story. So, we do not see the universe the way first-century Christians did, but we certainly can see ourselves "sort of like" that in a world where Christ has come and Christ will come again. This is not an interim ethic that can be dismissed by the modern story, but rather a call to follow Christ.

As such, this is very good news to working-class Americans. It turns the world of the principalities and powers on its head. It embraces a yearning that burns in resistance for another story, another history of the world. For those who seek an exit from this life it offers a different story with which to engage this life. For those who seek a populist anarchism, it offers an anarchism of another kind where duty ultimately is to God. It not only says to those who resist "you are not crazy," but gathers that resistance in a larger story that gives it more gravity than some nihilistic grunt that can only say "fuck 'em."

The Craft Tradition of Discipleship

In the craft use of Scripture the local church becomes the family of God, the community of interpretation that reads the biblical text like a trade journal from whence one learns the story of the craft and finds the skills and practices that embody the trade. The very reading itself requires skills that are not discovered somewhere and then applied to the text, but rather are the learning of a flesh and blood community that finds its life always already in a socially embodied tradition extended in time that works with the Bible as its central tool.

Chapter 7

THE SOCIAL WITNESS OF THE WHITE WORKING-CLASS CHURCH

So where does this leave us in terms of the social witness of the church? Let's review: the church needs to place its life in the midst of the practices of class with its liturgies of inequality. It will self-empty its practices of affluent taste, bourgeois etiquette, dominant language, and the grammar of privilege, and pitch tent with the practices of resistance found in working-class life. These indigenous practices, however, will be placed in a larger narrative of what God has done in calling out a new community in ancient Israel, in the incarnation of God in Jesus Christ, and in the new community of the church under the guidance of the Holy Spirit. Further, the church will respond to the religious practices of working people with a craft tradition of discipleship, apprenticeship learning, and a craft use of Scripture. What can we then say about how this will look in the church's social witness?

Worship as Social Witness

The first, and perhaps most important, social witness will be in worship: the liturgies of the gathering of the body of Christ, of proclamation, of Eucharist, and of being sent forth to the world God loves. No social witness of the church can begin anywhere else. It is here that we are formed in God's story, not only by hearing it but by enacting that story in praise, confession, prayer, affirmation, biblical reading, preaching, baptism, Eucharist, and in being sent forth. These are the practices that are central to the building of the body. Alexander Schmemann, an orthodox theologian, observes that the original meaning of *leitourgia* ("liturgy") "was an action by which a group of people become something corporately which they had not been as a mere collection of individuals." [1]

Worship in the working-class church, furthermore, will be more hospitable to those usually excluded from formal services that speak more to the college trained and their emotional restraint. It will be less "printy," but by this, not less focused in God's story. It will make greater use of oral practices such as call-and-response and lining out songs and other liturgical acts. Where indigenous it will make use of technology and multisensory and multimedia expression. [2] It will be an alternative to the middle-class forms of worship in the very nature of its oral and electronic practices. By the action of its worship it will be exemplary of a church that embodies the message that working people are God's people, both in the integrity of the worship and in its indigenous character.

The Eucharist itself will be an act of resistance and a basic form of joining working-class resistance. In the space generated by the body of Christ, the Eucharist enacts a radically different story than that of the principalities and powers. Here the people of God are invited to the table. No one has a special place. All are fed. The bread of heaven and the cup of salvation are shared equally by all. In the Eucharist the divisions of class, the fractures of the economic order, and the borders of the nation-states of the world are subverted. The walls of hostility are breached by the reconciling activity of Christ, and should be so interpreted. Living between the times, we enact this reconciled reality in eucharistic performance. This is an embodied practice. The people of God gather in the promise that, as they gather, Christ will be with them. We know him in the breaking of bread. In this act the Eucharist does not represent a reality that stands behind the event but rather enacts a reality that resides in it. "Christ does not lie behind the eucharistic sign but saturates it. Christians do not simply read the sign but perform it. We become Christ's body in the Eucharist." [3]

This means that the Eucharist is much more than a mere "memorial" service. Such understandings have done much to kill the power and the reality of the Eucharist for so many people. Working people need to understand that in their fragmented and busted up lives that when they come together in the Eucharist they *become* the body of Christ. There *is* a transubstantiation here, not of the accidents of bread and wine, but of the move from broken individuals to the corporate body. This is no mere consubstantiation, this is a changed reality. This is embodied, incorporated enactment. And here, as Christ has promised, Christ is present in radical objective relation and participative event.

I realize that the Eucharist often does not have the importance among working-class Protestants that I propose here. There are a number of reasons why this is so. The first is that most services of the Eucharist are so "printy" and too long. We wear them out with such things. A briefer service that makes use of the words of institution, a prayer, and a more active role for the congregation in distributing and receiving the elements is the direction the liturgy needs to go. Moreover, greater use of the Scripture in interpreting the Eucharist will help immensely. Finally, more connections with the daily life of working people will give them a deeper sense of the reach of the Eucharist into their lives. Here, the metaphor of the church as family provides an important resource—coming as it does from the extended family networks of working people—and offers a way to see the church as our more encompassing family and the Eucharist as the gathered embodiment of the family of Christ in sharing bread and cup.

Furthermore, the spaces in which the Eucharist is enacted may be especially important and are not to be limited to church buildings. John Wesley took the Eucharist to the fields to serve the working people of England. So I see a place here for offering the

Eucharist at appropriate spaces in the places of the principalities and powers. In some cases it will be on the street outside the church where working people are alienated from a congregation that has previously been closed or inhospitable. It may be offered in cases where a strike is going on or where there is a festival or where violence has occurred or may be imminent or where a plant has been closed or jobs outsourced or any number of other events where dividing walls of hostility have been built. It may be offered in a public park where homeless people gather who are too suspicious of a church building to go inside. Here the Eucharist is offered on the "tops of those walls." The point here, as William T. Cavanaugh has said, is "not to politicize the Eucharist but to 'Eucharistize' the world."[4]

Some in Protestant churches will maintain that working people will not respond to a church that practices the Eucharist regularly. This is decidedly not my experience. While it is true that a wordy, printy, and long service of Holy Communion will turn away almost all people, the Eucharist can become the most important and most powerful event in worship. In this connection Richard Lischer tells the wonderful story of a priest in North Carolina who began serving the Eucharist in a laundromat where Mexican workers gathered. They began with a half-dozen participants, but over time "the numbers grew modestly until soon many were gathering there from various parts of the county." They had come to worship. While these were Catholic workers, the far more important fact lies in this priest's offering of the Eucharist outside the church building and in the laundromat.[5]

Let the Church Be the Church

It is difficult in this context to exaggerate the importance of the church being the church, not because it is effective, but because without it we betray Christ. We are not called to be serpentine—only *wise* as serpents— we are called to be gentle as doves. Though we ought not turn this teaching into an absolute, since Christ himself was hardly gentle in cleansing the temple. Yet, he was not violent.[6] The serpentine is not to become the character of the church. Yet, this does not mean there is to be no consideration of moves to be taken. Yoder, for example, argues that the social witness of the church must be ad hoc, suggesting by this four things: (a) its unsystematic nature, (b) taking on one issue at a time, (c) usually assuming a negative approach, and (d) coming out of the life of the church. While there is a serpentine wisdom in these, they are not to become absolutes.[7]

But let me defend the import of Yoder's stance here. I was in a meeting with the chief of staff of one of our Arizona U.S. Senators this week. I was a part of the Valley Interfaith Project, a community organizing effort throughout the state. We were discussing the undocumented immigration of Mexican people into the U.S. The handling of this issue legally and otherwise is clearly broken. We were arguing for a more humane approach to people who are undocumented and to address the large numbers of people dying in the desert while trying to come across the border and avoid authorities. This is the major issue being addressed by the VIP presently.

As I sat there I reflected on Yoder's approach to social witness. As a group we had no idealized vision of how the society as a whole needed to be (we were not systematic). This is the major issue that VIP currently addresses (dealing here with one issue). We did not argue that we knew exactly what needed to be done; we just knew the system was broken and needed to be fixed (largely a negative approach in Yoder's sense). And the concerns of people in the room grew out of their faith convictions and the terrible inhospitality and resulting deaths of current policy. A good many of us believed that the church cannot draw a line on the earth and tell people in need that they cannot cross it. But it was more than having "a position." As I looked around that room, it was filled with a great variety of people: a diversity of racial ethnic groups including white working-class folk, a situation that required translators working in both English and Spanish, and people who were obviously affluent, those who were poor, and those in between. The group itself was such an intrinsic witness to a different reality than the one we now have at the borders of the U.S. There was no way a politician—though the chief of staff could not have been more receptive—could tell us we were naive or uninformed or not aware of the complexities of the issue. This interfaith group, by the very being of who it is, becomes the action. Nothing the group could have said or done had the impact of its identity. Here is one of the great strengths of Yoder's approach.

So I think here of churches who are made up of working-class people and who live down on the ground in their lives, who speak from what they know, and who, because of the integrity of their ministry and witness, have that concretely informed, practiced substance of life with working people. No politician can counter the claims of church witness like this. To be sure, the state can kill such people—see the Pinochet regime in Chile—but neither the state nor the other powers can finally overcome this kind of witness.

An Alternative Justice

When the church is the church, it offers a very different range of practices of justice than the more abstract kind now operative in the United States. In this country justice has become justice of a more formal kind. It is reduced to human rights and lacks a substantive commitment to the good. Justice is reduced to procedural rules that allow individuals to pursue their self-interests so long as they grant the same rights to others to do the same. This provides only the thinnest kind of commitment to the common good. When someone is challenged about conduct that is self-serving or narrowly conceived, the response often is, "Don't I have a right to do it?" This is a major source of the fragmentation of our culture and its loss of commitment to the good.

More than that, as Sheldon S. Wolin has argued, this approach to justice in the superpower that is now the United States deflects people from the destruction of politics happening in U.S. life. We now live in what Wolin calls an "inverted totalitarianism" where the citizen has been depoliticized, where corporate power contributes to fear and depoliticization through downsizing, outsourcing, and reduced pensions and health care, where "corporate power has become predominant in the political establishment," where totalizing regimes develop "an ideologically driven party with mass support," and where propaganda is advanced through "research universities" that have become "interlocked with corporate interests and with the propaganda machines represented by well-funded think tanks and conservative foundations." Added to this is the "virtual disappearance" of challenging criticism from the press and media.[8]

When a people is caught in the machinations of such a political economy, the idea of so-called free autonomous individuals pursuing their self-interests in an abstract set of rights is a blind acquiescence to the principalities and powers that has lost its commitment to a common good. In this context Wolin argues that the citizen has become consumer.

> The new economies created by technologically advanced societies provide equivalents for democracy's values of participation (mass consumption), inclusion (work force), and mass empowerment ("consumer sovereignty," "shareholder democracy").[9]

Wolin's response to the inverted totalitarianism of the superpower is a call to a "politics of the needs and aspirations of the Many." It is a democracy of forms rather than one of a form or constitution. Its focus is on those excluded and exploited. This alternative politics is one of "moments of experience" rather than "institutional processes." It is moments of "a crystallized response to deeply felt grievances or needs on the part of those whose main preoccupation . . . is to scratch out a decent existence."[10] He sees these as "small scale," the only size commensurate with the imposed limitations of our current political economy. Such sites must take a multiplicity of sites [spaces] and forms in "schools, community health services, police and fire protection, recreation, cultural institutions, property taxes." Such multiplicity is "anti-totality politics" constituted of "improvisation" and "anathema to centralization." Wolin observes that "resistance to the state" has typically originated not from the metropolitan center but from localities, states, and regions, a circumstance that fits in with his politics of the many.

My point in turning to Wolin here is not to prove that a politics of Jesus is relevant and effective. We engage in a politics of Jesus because it is faithful. My point rather is aimed at those who see the response outlined here as "sectarian" and irrelevant. When I listen to some theologians and ethicists, it seems as though they believe they have access to the ears of the powerful, indeed, that their "realism" or "more responsible" position is the one that really addresses our situation and is taken seriously by the superpower. Hardly.

The theologians, ethicists, and preachers who are visible and effective with inverted totalitarianism are those who pick out a few moral positions that represent no threat to the superpower but merely help round up votes in the electoral alliance of corporate interests, reactionaries, fundamentalists, right-wing ideologues, and some traditionalists. The church as tactic is a faithful alternative to such idolatry.

The implications of shifts toward inverted totalitarianism like these for working class churches are obvious. This is again an important site at which the church can be an alternative to the world. The reign of God is the good of the church and is the informing vision and aim of its life. While the church will always be an inadequate and imperfect expression of that rule, it is nonetheless called to make that witness visible in its life. The church's persistence in offering a different justice that is inseparable from the good of God's reign is intrinsic to its witness. It is, too, a radically different justice than that of self-seeking individuals merely claiming mutual rights and naked of any wider commitment to the good of all.

Furthermore, as William Cavanaugh has demonstrated, justice as rights without a larger conception of the good atomizes people into individuals. The state takes the rich, vibrant life of a great range of social groups and transfers power from civil society to the state as a whole. Then, when it is the state itself that is violating human rights, where can one appeal? When the state is called upon to protect the individual from its own self-interest, who is more likely to prevail?[11]

Let me be clear, however, I do not mean to suggest that attention to human rights is unimportant. They are now a diminishing set of claims that people can use against the growing encroachments of the nation-state and capitalism. At the same time, basic to the church's resistance and to its "outnarrating" the world is its witness to power in this larger framework of the crucial relationship of justice to the common good. The case for the rightful claims of people against the emergent forms of inverted totalitarianism will finally be dependent on a commitment to the common good rather than upon rights abstractly conceived and fulfilled primarily in consumer activity. The surfacing of this commitment is far more likely to come from a politics of the many than from "responsible voices" seeking the ear of dominant power.

The Common Good and Other Faith Traditions

So far I have not discussed other traditions, especially faith traditions. How is the church to relate to them, especially in pursuits of the common good? The first thing is to see the necessity of relating to other faith traditions as a fundamental duty of the church. In both the Old Testament and the New Testament the stranger, the other, receives a great deal of attention. The instructions of hospitality are strong and clear. In the New Testament we learn that the stranger or the other is our neighbor, that they may be angels of whom we are unaware, and most important that they may be

Christ himself. I cannot imagine that the God we know in Jesus Christ is not active in other faith traditions, and we cannot know ahead of time what God is doing through other traditions. Hence hospitality to other faiths is intrinsic to the church's life.

It has been my good fortune to participate in the Arizona Interfaith Movement (AIM) over the last two years. It has been a valuable experience. Two things stand out especially in our work. One is that each tradition, and there are twenty-three traditions represented in the Movement, is to be heard with respect. It is an occasion of listening. Opportunities to "overhear" other traditions are rich opportunities to attend to affirmations of faith that often are truly other. It has enriched my sense of God's action in other communities. Second, when people are asked to pray or speak, they are asked to speak quite decidedly out of their own tradition. I have found this to be no little relief from my experience in too many contexts where others are so often attempting to turn diverse traditions into some abstract, generalized universal religion or some mere morality.

This experience with AIM renews my sense that this kind of listening and this kind of attention to the particularity of each tradition is a way to move beyond some formal justice composed of mere procedural rules for the pursuit of self-interest. My hope is that AIM can turn its attention to the matter of the common good. One thing the group does already that is an important move is to take actions together. When an act of religious intolerance is committed in the city, the group gathers at the site of the violation in support of the transgressed parties; for example, in one case it was the home of a Sikh who had been killed; in another case it was a mosque that had been burned. These acts of care and of solidarity with the other are the building block practices of interfaith searches for the common good. We do not know where these go yet, but they offer ways to work together that respect the integrity of the various traditions and look for common cause together.

This is an important direction for the working-class church as well. The focus on practices of listening and acts of support and solidarity bring into play a craft of care. These are not merely intellectual activities of writing papers and theological affirmations, but get the action down on the ground where things are done, and where knowing resides in knowing how to care and what to do.

Populist Anarchism and Constantinianism

In the pages above I describe a populist anarchism among the working class. Not a classical anarchism nor a stereotypical one of bomb-throwing cartoon figures, it is rather one that loves country and distrusts government and yearns to be free from the institutional constraints of the modern world. Not politically programmatic or committed to specific social policy, it is resistant to social control and regards the formal legal system as suspect. Talk of theory, theorists, fine print, and fancy double-talk identifies the bearers of such things as the enemy or at the very least, not on the side of working people.

Quite frankly, there is a good deal I appreciate about populist anarchism because it has no little realism about what working people are up against with the government and a host of people who have agendas that are antithetical to their lives. At the same time, such attitudes and commitments can lead to a withdrawal of working people from their roles as citizens working in behalf of the common good. For this reason among others, populist anarchism needs to be placed in a different narration, and the church can do this.

In the church the energy of populist anarchism needs a better focus and a different formation. Let me say, however, that in terms of love of country and distrust of government, I think that's not altogether bad. There is an altogether appropriate love of country when it is not seduced into idolatry. And distrust of government is a fruitful ground for addressing "the heresy of Constantinianism" in the words of Yoder.[12] For Yoder, Constantinianism is a heresy that rejects or distorts the eschatology of the New Testament. To put it another way, it denies or distorts or privatizes or idealizes the story of God as we know it in Jesus Christ. It denies the lordship of Christ when the state takes the place of Christ or modifies or replaces commitment to his lordship. Constantinianism denies the two-age character of the church's story where the church lives in the tension of the "already" and the "not yet." Christ has come; Christ will come again. In Constantinianism the story of the state becomes the story of the world and the state becomes the bearer of the meaning of history. Further, the state can arrogate unto itself the role of the kingdom of God. While many nation-states would not say it in these terms, nationalism often spiritualizes faith tradition, giving it a status that has little if any empirical reality in the affairs of that society. Yet, further, in the Constantinian state the tension between the church and the world is often collapsed so that, for example, being a good American and being a good Christian are identified, and the church loses its tension with the world.

My sum here is but an abstract and too simple statement of Yoder's critique of Constantinianism, but perhaps it will suggest something of the sweep of his view. It is a call for the church to be the church and not to be swept up into the story of the state at the expense of the story of God in Christ. Distrust of the state, though not withdrawal from citizenship, in the light of these considerations, is a good thing.

Let me be clear, my hope here is not that of a theocratic state. I do not want the Ten Commandments put up in courthouses, nor do I want prayer in public schools, and I have no wish to wrap the cross in the American flag. The last thing we need is to have the state or public schools writing "harmless" prayers or prayers to some deity in general, and we do not need to legitimate the most powerful nation on earth with the symbols of Christian faith. In the church the state needs to be seen for what it is in the New Testament, one of the powers created to be good, but fallen, and to be redeemed in the coming of the reign of God in history. In the meanwhile, as Alasdair MacIntyre says, we need to treat the government like the telephone company: as a large bureaucracy that promises more than it can deliver. MacIntyre, moreover, notes that the state sees itself as a "repository of sacred values, which from time to time invites one to lay down one's life on its behalf . . . it is like being asked to die for the telephone company."[13]

The Peaceable Church

I come now to the most difficult commitment for the church to make in North America, to be a nonviolent community because of the revelation of God in Jesus Christ. This is no less true for the working-class church than for any other. Yet, I will argue it is central to the social witness of a faithful church. Basic to the problem is the church's commitment to the story of the nation-state. The state's story is typically the operative power in church life. We continually place the story of Jesus Christ in the story of the nation-state and move to arguments of the "just" war, the "interim ethic" of the New Testament, or the use of the love commandment to protect innocent victims.[14] No one has done more damage to the church's nonviolent witness in the last century than Reinhold Niebuhr, whose career did more to write an ethic for the nation-state than for the church.

It is not my aim here to write an ethic for the nation-state. Rather, my aim is to suggest an ethic for the church. I do not expect the nation-state to be nonviolent. Charles Tilly and a number of other scholars find as a result of their studies that the building of the modern nation-state historically depends on war. The capacity of state-making elites to do war required a capacity to extract resources, which required a state bureaucracy to obtain them from a resistive population. They conclude, "War made the state and the state made war." In his study of the role of war in state building, Michael Howard says it clearly: "The entire apparatus of the state primarily came into being to enable princes to wage war." The findings of these scholars are not that war is the single cause of state building. Perhaps William Cavanaugh says it most succinctly and accurately in a sum of the work of Bruce Porter: "War was the catalyst and *sine qua non* mobilizing the other factors in the formation of the state."[15] There were, of course, wars prior to the modern nation-state, but the institution of war is itself historically conditioned and varies across time, that is, the institution of war was different. My point, however, is that war is endemic to the nation-state.

I need also to make a comment about war and the working class. The people who do most of the fighting and most of the dying (with the exception of civilians in most cases), are the working class: black, white, red, gold, and brown. No one should be more suspicious of the war making of the nation-state than people in the lower classes. Yet, the power of nationalism is such that often these very classes are the most patriotic and the most prepared to give up their bodies to the state.

To resist this kind of nationalism will not likely occur by rationally arguing the history of the nation-state and war or the unfairness of the sacrifices made in its behalf. My argument instead has to do with a position that is intrinsic to the faith. It is not an argument based on effectiveness or on long-range consequences. It is based on the story of Christ as we have it in the New Testament.

The pacifism of the church is based in the story of Christ as the Word made flesh, as the Messiah of God who has come and established the messianic community of the church. Yoder states, "If Jesus Christ was not who historic Christianity confesses he was, the revelation in the life of a real man of the character of God himself, then this one argument for pacifism collapses."[16] This means that his argument for pacifism hangs utterly on the incarnation. Yoder, for example, does not make his case for pacifism on the basis of principles or rules. In his *The Politics of Jesus* he never quotes the line from Matthew, "If anyone strikes you on the right cheek, turn the other also" (5:39). Further, he does not extract principles from the gospels or the letters so they can be "applied." Such moves leave too much room for one to wiggle away from the fuller impact of the incarnation itself. This does not exclude the teaching of Jesus, but is a great deal more than that teaching taken alone. Yoder says of the Incarnation:

The business of ethical thinking has been taken away from the speculation of independent minds each meditating on the meaning of things and has been pegged to a particular set of answers given in a particular time and place. . . . [The] will of God is affirmatively, concretely knowable in the person and ministry of Jesus.[17]

Central to the incarnation on Yoder's view is the cross. In his death we see Christ, and therefore God, not oppose the powers, but give himself up to them. He does not resist their mockery, torture, abuse, and legal "court recourse"—not even the suffocating agony of the cross—but rather reveals their lack of ultimacy in his submission and finally in his resurrection. In crucifixion and resurrection God is made known in the character of his dealing with us.

Richard Hays, also, maintains that the New Testament must be read through the focal lens of the cross. Thinking about ethics requires that the death of Jesus move "to the center of our attention." We must not simply search the text for "principles (the imperative of justice) or prooftexts ('I have not come to bring peace but a sword'): rather all such principles and texts must be interpreted in light of the story of the cross."[18]

This story of the cross is not often preached in working-class churches so far as I can tell. Yet, I believe it can be heard. The search for authentic faith as expressed in practices of believing and feeling indicates a serious concern for a relationship with God. The struggle for a trust in God and an assurance of God's presence in times of struggle and coping are lures to a more dedicated discipleship. The hardness of much of working-class life itself can lead to identification with Christ on the cross. These and the energy of a populist anarchism can move in the direction of a politics of Jesus understood in these terms.

Such moves will require no little naming of the relationship of the nation-state to war, of the uneven sacrifices made by working people, and of the role of the church as the body of Christ. But these are not enough. Nothing can substitute for the witness to the incarnation in the church itself. This can occur in congregations that begin with the practices of nonviolent life. As I write, the United States is involved in an unjust war in Iraq. I would love to see large numbers of young people in working-class churches (and in others, of course) taking the equivalent of conscientious objector status. I wish for Christian pacifists of long commitment to be teaching and mentoring young apprentices in how to be peaceable, helping them know how to enact a politics of the cross. I can imagine few witnesses more important for the church that once again populates "Rome."

The church as the body of Christ is called to a self-emptying, a pitching of tent in the working-class world, an emptying of class posturing, a casting aside of the subtleties of a politics of distinction, and a refusal of the rituals of inequality. Called out to live lives formed by the radical sharing of bread and wine in the Eucharist, the church opposes the distortions of the official world—the principalities and powers. Where lives caught in the rituals of class are countered by a congregation of hospitality and mutual respect; where a community of faith becomes a free zone, an open space in a culture of class captivity; where the valuations of the world are turned upside down; where the self-elevations of supremacist tastes, language, etiquette, affect, and lifestyles are countered by an honoring of indigenous practices; where the church itself is a community of resistance against the external impositions and lifestyle colonialism of the dominant order; and where the idols of class are met with an anarchism committed to Christ, there the church lives out God's story as an alternative people of embodied practices intrinsic to the reign of God. This church as tactic engaged in the craft of discipleship will be a foretaste of the reign of God, albeit in broken and imperfect ways. This church will be a social witness by its very existence as a worshiping community. This church can testify to an alternative justice of the common good. This church can reach out to others as neighbors, angels, and Christ himself, to learn again and again what God is about in the world. This church can be peaceable and embody the truth of its crucified and risen Lord.

NOTES

CHAPTER ONE: PITCHING TENT IN THE WORLD OF CLASS

1. I am indebted to Gustavo Gutiérrez for first pointing this out to me in his *Theology of Liberation: History, Politics, and Salvation*, trans. and ed. Sister Caridad Inda and John Eagleson (Maryknoll, N.Y.: Orbis Books, 1973), 192f. See too Gutiérrez's report of the ministry of Bartolome de Las Casas in *Las Casas: In Search of the Poor in Jesus Christ*, trans. Robert R. Barr (Maryknoll, N.Y.: Orbis Books, 1995), especially chapter 3, "If We Were Indian."

2. Coe's distinction appears in Ruy O. Costa, ed., *One Faith, Many Cultures* (Maryknoll, N.Y.: Orbis Books, 1988), xii. I am indebted to Alan Neely for drawing my attention to this. See his very helpful book *Christian Mission: A Case Study Approach* (Maryknoll, N.Y.: Orbis Books, 1995), 8. My position, however, does not reflect his own.

3. For further reading on the trends I summarize here, see: Stanley Aronowitz and William DiFazio, *The Jobless Future: Sci-Tech and the Dogma of Work* (Minneapolis: University of Minnesota Press, 1994); Bill Bamberger and Cathy Davidson, *Closing: The Life and Death of an American Factory* (New York, N.Y.: Doubleday/ Norton, 1998); Kathleen Barker and Kathleen Christensen, eds., *Contingent Work: American Employment Relations in Transition* (Ithaca: ILR Press, 1998); Donald L. Barlett and James B. Steele, *America: Who Stole the Dream?* (Kansas City: Andrews and McMeel, 1996); Kathryn Edin and Laura Lein, *Making Ends Meet: How Single Mothers Survive Welfare and Low-Wage Work* (New York: Russell Sage Foundation, 1997); William Finnegan, *Cold New World: Growing Up in a Harder Country* (New York: Random House, 1998); Frederic L. Pryor and David L. Schaffer, *Who's Not Working and Why: Employment,*

Cognitive Skills, Wages, and the Changing U.S. Labor Market (New York: Cambridge University Press, 1999); Richard Sennett, *The Corrosion of Character: The Personal Consequences of Work in the New Capitalism* (New York: W. W. Norton, 1998); Juliet B. Schor, *The Overworked American: The Unexpected Decline of Leisure* (New York: Basic Books, 1992); John E. Schwarz, *Illusions of Opportunity: The American Dream in Question* (New York: W. W. Norton, 1998); John E. Schwarz and Thomas J. Volgy, *The Forgotten Americans: Thirty Million Working Poor in the Land of Opportunity* (New York: W. W. Norton, 1992); William Julius Wilson, *When Work Disappears: The World of the New Urban Poor* (New York: Alfred A. Knopf, 1996).

4. Manuel Castells, in his three-volume work *The Network Society*, contends that the basic problem is not the skills of working people but the distribution of income and wealth. Manuel Castells, *The Network Society*, vol. 1 (London: Blackwell Publishers, 1996), 273-74.

5. Barbara Ehrenreich, *Nickel and Dimed: On (Not) Getting By in America* (New York: Henry Holt and Company, 2001), 213.

6. *The Network Society*, vol. 1, 64-168.

CHAPTER TWO: THE PRACTICES OF CLASS

1. E. P. Thompson, *The Making of the English Working Class* (Hammondsworth: Penguin Books, 1980), 8-9.

2. Goffman's classic statement on such interaction rituals is *The Presentation of the Self in Everyday Life* (Garden City, N.Y.: Doubleday Anchor Books, 1959). Let me say, however, that if one is to define class it cannot be done without Marx who in his classic position saw class as the relationship one has to the material means of production, that is, as one who owns the means of production (the bourgeoisie) or as with labor who have nothing to sell but their labor (the proletariat). I am working with class in this book, however, in terms of its practices, hence the focus I use here. For a brief but fine overview of Marx's position on class, see Anthony Giddens, *Capitalism and Modern Social Theory: An Analysis of the Writings of Marx, Durkheim, and Max Weber* (Cambridge: Cambridge University Press, 1971), 35-45.

3. Randall Collins makes use of Goffman in his *Conflict Sociology: Toward an Explanatory Science* (New York: Academic Press, 1975), chapters 2–4.

4. Lawrence W. Levine, *Highbrow/Lowbrow: The Emergence of Cultural Hierarchy in America* (Cambridge: Harvard University Press, 1988), 221-23.

5. Tex Sample, *White Soul: Country Music, the Church, and Working Americans* (Nashville: Abingdon Press, 1996), 41-54.

6. DiMaggio, "Cultural Entrepreneurship in Nineteenth-century Boston: The Creation of an Organizational Base of High Culture in America," *Media, Culture and Society* 4, no. 1 (1982): 34.

7. Levine, *Highbrow/Lowbrow*, 221-23.

8. Robert Walser, "Highbrow, Lowbrow, Voodoo Aesthetics," in Andrew Ross and Tricia Rose, eds. *Microphone Fiends: Youth Music and Youth Culture* (London: Routledge, 1994), 235.

9. Immanuel Kant, *Critique of Judgment*, quoted in Carl J. Friedrich, ed., *The Philosophy of Kant*, trans. J. C. Meredith (New York: The Modern Library, 1949), 284-307.

10. Giacomo Puccini, the libretto of *La Boheme*, by Puccini and Luigi Illica (London: G. Ricordi & Co., 1973), 32-36.

11. Immanuel Kant, *Critique of Judgment*, trans. J. C. Meredith (London: Oxford University Press, 1952), 65.

12. Bob McDill, Wayland Holyfield, and Chuck Neese, "Rednecks, White Socks, and Blue Ribbon Beer." Copyright 1973 Jack Music Inc. and Jando Music, Inc., and Mary Chapin Carpenter, "Down at the Twist and Shout." Copyright 1990 EMI April Music Inc. and Getarealjob Music.

13. "Soliloquy," *Carousel*. Copyright 1945 Williamson Music Co. In this connection see feminist criticisms of classical music as disembodied: Hilde Hein, "Refining Feminist Theory," in Hein and Carolyn Korsmeyer, eds., *Aesthetics in Feminist Perspective* (Bloomington: Indiana University Press, 1993), 9-13. Susan McClary claims "classical music is perhaps our cultural medium most centrally concerned with the denial of the body." *Feminine Endings: Music, Gender, and Sexuality* (Minneapolis: University of Minnesota Press, 1991), 79, see 54.

14. Pierre Bourdieu, *Distinction: A Social Critique of the Judgment of Taste*, trans. Richard Nice (Cambridge: Harvard University

Press, 1984), 491. Bourdieu's work is an extraordinary account of the relationship of class to taste. I am indebted to him throughout this section.

CHAPTER THREE: THE PRACTICES OF RESISTANCE

1. John Fisk, *Understanding Popular Culture* (London: Hyman, 1989), 8, 20-21.
2. Pierre Bourdieu, *Language and Symbolic Power* (Cambridge: Harvard University Press, 1991), 88.
3. Ibid.
4. Michel de Certeau, *The Practice of Everyday Life*, trans. Steven Rendall (Berkeley: University of California Press, 1984), xix.
5. I am indebted to Elaine Lawless and Teresa Stewart for telling me these stories. These particular stories of Wilson are not in print so far as Lawless and Stewart know. However, there is an article by Wilson on the Internet that has similar material. See: http://weberstudies.weber.edu/archive/archive%20B%20Vol.%2011-16.1/Vol.%2013.1/13.1Wilson.htm
6. James C. Scott, "Weapons of the Weak: Everyday Struggle, Meaning, and Deeds," in Teodor Shanin ed., *Peasants and Peasant Societies*, 2d ed. (Oxford: Basil Blackwell, 1987), 319. See the fuller statement of this work in James C. Scott's *Domination and the Arts of Resistance: Hidden Transcripts* (New Haven: Yale University Press, 1990).
7. Mikhail Bakhtin, *Rabelais and His World*, trans. Hélène Iswolsky (Bloomington, Indiana: Indiana University Press, 1984), 196-276, see especially 261-76.
8. This outline is my abstract summary of Klatch's much more detailed and rich statement. See Rebecca Klatch, *Women of the New Right* (Philadelphia: Temple University Press, 1987), 20-54.
9. James M. Ault Jr., "Family and Fundamentalism: The Shawmut Valley Baptist Church," in Jim Obelkevich, Lyndal Roper, and Raphael Samuel, eds., *Disciplines of Faith* (London: Routledge & Kegan Paul, 1987), 13-36. See his fuller treatment of this church and its life in his wonderful *Spirit and Flesh: Life in a Fundamentalist Baptist Church* (New York: Alfred A. Knopf, 2004).

10. Ed Bruce and Patsy Bruce, Waylon Jennings, Willie Nelson, "Mammas, Don't Let Your Babies Grow Up to Be Cowboys," © 1978 RCA.
11. Mikhail Bakhtin, *Rabelais and His World*, trans. Hélène Iswolsky (Bloomington, Ind.: Indiana University Press, 1984), 275.
12. Ault, *Spirit and Flesh*, 202.
13. Ibid., 99.
14. Ibid., 197.
15. Ibid., 197.
16. *Blue Collar Ministry* (Valley Forge: Judson Press, 1984), 71-84. See also part III in my *U.S. Lifestyles and Mainline Churches* (Louisville: Westminster/John Knox, 1990), and *Ministry in an Oral Culture* (Louisville: Westminster/John Knox, 1994), 29-44.
17. Tex Sample, *Hard Living People and Mainstream Christians* (Nashville: Abingdon Press), 61-74.

CHAPTER FOUR: FAITH COMMITMENT OF THE HEART

1. See my *Ministry in an Oral Culture: Living with Will Rogers, Uncle Remus, and Minnie Pearl* (Louisville: Westminster, 1994) for a fuller treatment of these issues.
2. James Ault Jr., *Spirit and Flesh: Life in a Fundamentalist Baptist Church* (New York: Alfred A. Knopf, 2004), 194.
3. Ibid., 195.
4. This is Tony Pappas's very helpful phrase from his book *Entering the World of the Small Church: A Guide for Leaders* (Washington, D.C.: Alban Institute, 1988).
5. Walter J. Ong, *Orality and Literacy: The Technologizing of the Word* (London: Routledge, 1982), 11, 136-38.
6. Leonard Sweet, *Faithquakes* (Nashville: Abingdon Press, 1994), 41-68.
7. I address these issues, though not explicitly along the lines of class, in *The Spectacle of Worship in a Wired World: Electronic Culture and the Gathered People of God* (Nashville: Abingdon Press, 1998) and in my *Powerful Persuasion: Multimedia Witness in Christian Worship* (Nashville: Abingdon Press, 2005).
8. More than a few studies suggest that workers find ways on the job to make it "better" and to bring life to the work. See for

example Kathryn Marie Dudley, *The End of the Line* (Chicago: University of Chicago Press, 1994), 116-34.

CHAPTER FIVE: THE POLITICS OF JESUS

1. Richard B. Hays, *The Moral Vision of the New Testament* (San Francisco: HarperSanFrancisco, 1996), 161-64.
2. John Howard Yoder, *The Politics of Jesus* (Grand Rapids: Eerdmans, 1972), 237, 249.
3. John Howard Yoder, *The Royal Priesthood: Essays Ecclesiological and Ecumenical*, ed. Michael G. Cartwright (Grand Rapids: Eerdmanns, 1994), 73-75, 80-81.
4. Michel de Certeau, *The Practice of Everyday Life* (Berkeley: University of California Press, 1984), 36.
5. Ibid., 37.
6. Ibid., 38.
7. Kathryn Marie Dudley, *The End of the Line* (Chicago: University of Chicago Press, 1994), 120.
8. I am indebted in this paragraph to Robert Ratcliff for his comments, which helped me clarify the point made here. I am, of course, responsible for the final statement.
9. Stanley Hauerwas has discussed "living out of control" in very helpful ways in a good deal of his work. See *The Hauerwas Reader* (Durham, N.C.: Duke University Press, 2001), 380-82.
10. The more earthy term is a better translation of the Greek than the NRSV's "rubbish." I am indebted to Richard Hays for pointing out Paul's use of *skybala* in this passage. See his *The Moral Vision of the New Testament* (San Francisco: HarperSanFrancisco, 1996), 30 and 57, n. 39.
11. Dudley, *The End of the Line*, 152.
12. Stanley Hauerwas, *Sanctify Them in the Truth* (Nashville: Abingdon Press, 1998), 9.
13. Samuel Wells, *Improvisation: The Drama of Christian Ethics* (Grand Rapids: Brazos Press, 2004), 131, but see all of chapter 9.
14. Wynonna Judd, "Live with Jesus," *Wynonna* (Universal City, Ca.: Curb Music Co./MCA Records, 1992).

15. "The politics of Jesus" is John Howard Yoder's phrase and the title of his important book by that name, *The Politics of Jesus: Vicit, Agnus Noster* (Grand Rapids: Eerdmans, 1994). I am greatly influenced by Yoder in what follows.

16. Craig A. Carter, *The Politics of the Cross: The Theology and Social Ethics of John Howard Yoder* (Grand Rapids: Brazos Press, 2001), 220. Yoder does not do a systemic statement of his position because he was suspicious of such grand designs of thought, but Carter does a very nice overview of Yoder's work while remaining sensitive to Yoder's resistance to systematization.

17. I get the phrase "liturgies of status" from Samuel Wells's *Improvisation: The Drama of Christian Ethics* (Grand Rapids: Brazos Press, 2004), see 87-101.

CHAPTER SIX: THE CRAFT TRADITION OF DISCIPLESHIP

1. I am indebted here to Alasdair MacIntyre who makes this point in his *Three Rival Versions of Moral Enquiry: Encyclopaedia, Genealogy, and Tradition* (Notre Dame, Ind.: University of Notre Dame Press, 1990), 69. He states: "The philosophy of the craft-tradition presented the mind as inadequate until it had conformed itself to the object which theology presented for its attention." Later MacIntyre writes: "For the philosophy of craft-tradition, knowledge is a secondary phenomenon to be understood in the light of the objects of knowledge and not vice versa."

2. For a fine discussion of modernity and the Enlightenment, see Stephen Toulmin, *Cosmopolis: The Hidden Agenda of Modernity* (Chicago: University of Chicago Press, 1992).

3. I am grateful that a substantial critique of the Enlightenment is now occurring in the university. It will be interesting to see where this goes over the next hundred years.

4. Alasdair MacIntyre, *After Virtue* (Notre Dame, Ind.: University of Notre Dame Press, 1984), 222.

5. Stanley Hauerwas has stated this for some time.

6. I do not mean to suggest that all working people are open to a biblical faith. See David Halle's study of chemical workers in New Jersey who were mainly Catholic. Halle concludes from

his study that the categories and beliefs of Christianity aim to be of some relevance to most aspects of the world that concern these workers. But in the context of workers' actual beliefs, they end up as a structure of "secondary cosmologies" and "tertiary beliefs." Such a set of beliefs, which purports to explain more than one area of the world but falls short in all areas, can be called a "set of mediocre cosmologies." It would have been interesting for him to study more directly churches and working people in them, especially those not in the Catholic Church and mainline churches, which seem to be the focus of his attention. I mean here the so-called sectarian churches. See David Halle, *America's Working Man* (Chicago: University of Chicago Press, 1984), 253-69.

7. MacIntyre, *Three Rival Versions of Moral Enquiry*, 61-63. See also chapter IV.

8. Kathryn Marie Dudley, *The End of the Line* (Chicago: University of Chicago Press, 1994), 107.

9. I do not mean to suggest that all bosses are as unversed as the young engineer. There are, of course, many bosses in the oil field who are sagacious, experienced people who "know pipe." As such, however, they are people of the craft tradition.

10. See *The Hauerwas Reader*, edited by John Berkman and Michael Cartwright (Durham: Duke University Press, 2001), 183, 200, 207, 219, 245, 641, among many others.

11. See my *U.S. Lifestyles and Mainline Churches* (Louisville: Westminster/John Knox, 1990), 88-93.

12. John Yoder, "How to Be Read by the Bible" (Elkhart, Ind.: A Shalom Desktop Publication, 1996), 65. Quoted in Craig A. Carter, *The Politics of the Cross* (Grand Rapids: Brazos Press, 2001), 25-26, see note 34.

13. Stanley Hauerwas and Alex Sider make this point about Yoder's biblical realism in their introduction to Yoder's *Preface to Theology: Christology and Theological Method* (Grand Rapids: Brazos Press, 2002), 24f.

14. John Yoder, "How to Be Read by the Bible," 8.

15. Ibid., 13.

16. See Yoder, *The Priestly Kingdom: Social Ethics as Gospel* (Notre Dame, Ind.: Notre Dame University Press, 1984), 37.

17. John Yoder, "Armaments and Eschatology," *Studies in Christian Ethics* (T & T Clark, 1988), 51, quoted in Michael Cartwright's introduction, "Radical Reform, Radical Catholicity: John Howard Yoder's Vision of the Faithful Church," to the book Yoder, *The Royal Priesthood* (Grand Rapids: Eerdmans, 1994), 37-38.

18. Cartwright, "Radical Reform, Radical Catholicity," 38.

19. *The Royal Priesthood*, 353. A good deal is made of the difference between Yoder's view of Scripture and that of Stanley Hauerwas. I think the difference is not as great as some scholars suggest. Hauerwas, using the work of Stanley Fish, maintains that no one reads a text literally, but rather we read and interpret them as part of an interpreting community. At one point Hauerwas states flatly: "no 'text' can be substituted for the people of God." See Hauerwas, *Unleashing the Scripture* (Nashville: Abingdon Press, 1993), 28, but see 19-28. For a different reading of Yoder and Hauerwas on this point, see Richard Hays, *The Moral Vision of the New Testament* (San Francisco: HarperSanFrancisco, 1996), 239-65. See also Stanley Fish, *Is There a Text in this Class?: The Authority of Interpretive Communities* (Cambridge: Harvard University Press, 1980).

20. I do not mean to suggest here that the Bible as story is only good for working people. I would argue it is the way to work with the Bible as the church's book, but in working with, say, middle-class professionals, the connections would be different.

21. See Craig Carter's fine discussion of these matters in Yoder in his *The Politics of the Cross*, 219.

22. Eugene D. Genovese, *Roll, Jordan, Roll: The World the Slaves Made* (New York: Vintage Books, 1974).

23. See Lawrence W. Levine, *Black Culture and Black Consciousness: Afro-American Folk Thought from Slavery to Freedom* (New York: Oxford University Press, 1977), chapter 1. Steven D. Hoogerwerf makes important use of Genovese and Levine in his dissertation where he works on the role of resistance in the life of the church. See his "Forming the Character of Christian Discipleship: Singing the Lord's Song in a Strange Land" (unpublished Ph.D. diss., Duke University, 1991), 293-310. I am indebted to him for calling to my attention these connections.

24. *Worlds of Pain* is the title of Lillian Rubin's fine work on working-class life, *Worlds of Pain: Life in the Working-class Family* (New York; Basic Books, 1976). For a more recent treatment of the struggles of working-class women in their workaday lives see Barbara Ehrenreich, *Nickel and Dimed: On (Not) Getting by in America* (New York: Metropolitan Books, 2001).

25. I am indebted here to John Howard Yoder and his use of "analogical imagination." Yoder maintains that if we are to witness to Christ's Lordship in today's world the call is to renew in this language world of pluralism/relativism an "analogue to what those first transcultural reconceptualizers (i.e., the New Testament writers) did; not to translate their results but to emulate their exercise. What we need to find is the interworld transformational grammar to help us discern what will need to happen if the collision of the message of Jesus with our pluralist/relativist world is to lead to a reconception of the shape of the world, instead of rendering Jesus optional or innocuous." Such language as analogical imagination, however, will not be helpful in working-class congregations. It is not that they cannot understand the concept; it is that that kind of language is not only not part of their world; it will be seen as pretentious. See Yoder, *The Priestly Kingdom*, 56. I am indebted here to Richard Hays for calling my attention to this quote. See Hays, *The Moral Vision of the New Testament* (San Francisco: HarperSanFrancisco, 1996), 249.

26. Yoder, *The Priestly Kingdom*, 37f.

27. Albert Schweitzer, *The Quest of the Historical Jesus*, ed. John Bowden (Minneapolis: Fortress Press, 2001), 485-87.

CHAPTER SEVEN: THE SOCIAL WITNESS OF THE WHITE WORKING-CLASS CHURCH

1. Alexander Schmem, *For the Life of the World* (Crestwood, N.Y.: St. Vladimir's Seminary Press, 1988), 25. Quoted in William T. Cavanaugh, *Torture and Eucharist* (Malden, Mass.: Blackwell Publishers, 1998), 12.

2. I have addressed multimedia and multisensory practices of worship in two books: *The Spectacle of Worship in a Wired World* (Nashville: Abingdon Press, 1998) and *Powerful Persuasion* (Nashville: Abingdon Press, 2005).

3. Cavanaugh, *Torture and Eucharist*, 14.

4. Ibid.

5. "The Called Life: An Essay on the Pastoral Vocation," *Interpretation* 59, no. 2 (April 2005): 175. I am indebted to Robert Ratcliff for calling my attention to this article.

6. See Yoder, *The Politics of Jesus* (Grand Rapids: Eerdmans, 1972), 48-53.

7. I am indebted here, again, to Craig Carter's fine overview of Yoder's work. See *The Politics of the Cross* (Grand Rapids: Brazos Press, 2001), 209-12.

8. See Sheldon S. Wolin's compelling analysis of these matters in *Politics and Vision: Continuity and Innovation in Western Political Thought*, expanded ed. (Princeton: Princeton University Press, 2004), 590-95.

9. Ibid., 588.

10. Ibid., 603.

11. William T. Cavanaugh, *Theopolitical Imagination* (New York: T & T Clark, 2002), 43-46.

12. I do not have the space here to do a detailed summary of Yoder's view of Constantinianism, but Craig Carter has done a fine statement in his *The Politics of the Cross*, see chapter 6.

13. "A Partial Response to My Critics," in John Horton and Susan Mendus, ed. *After MacIntyre: Critical Perspectives on the Work of Alasdair MacIntyre* (Notre Dame, Ind.: University of Notre Dame Press, 1994), 303. See William Cavanaugh's development of MacIntyre's characterization in his "Killing for the Telephone Company: Why the Nation-State Is Not the Keeper of the Common Good," *Modern Theology* 20, no. 2 (April 2004): 243-74, especially page 263.

14. See Yoder, *The Politics of Jesus*, chapter 1, for his sum of the ways in which theologians and ethicists discount the life, teaching, death, and resurrection of Christ as a claim on the nonviolent witness of the church.

15. I am dependent here on William T. Cavanaugh's work on the nation-state. His gathering of the findings of the scholars to whom I refer deserves a wide reading and the most serious kind of reflection and response. See "Killing for the Telephone Company," 246-50, especially pages 249-50. Charles Tilly and

Michael Howard are quoted in Cavanaugh. See also his *Theopolitical Imagination*, Chapter 1.

16. *The Politics of Jesus*, 237.

17. Ibid., 233. I am indebted to Richard Hays for calling my attention to this quote and for making the observation that Yoder does not argue from derivative rules and principles. See his extraordinary discussion of Yoder in *The Moral Vision of the New Testament* (San Francisco: HarperSanFrancisco, 1996), 240-53, especially pages 248f. See also Hays's own biblical defense for a pacifist church in chapter 14. My appreciation for Hays's work on nonviolence should not be taken as agreement with his other stands in his book, especially his chapter on homosexuality.

18. *The Moral Vision of the New Testament*, 338. Hays's chapter "Violence in Defense of Justice" is influenced by Yoder, and worth a careful reading on its own merits.